Jorge Octavio Guzmán Sánchez

Enhanced Advanced Web Development

Jorge Octavio Guzmán Sánchez

Enhanced Advanced Web Development

We continue to add

ScienciaScripts

Imprint

Cover image: www.ingimage.com

This book is a translation from the original published under ISBN 978-620-2-12507-9.

Publisher:
Sciencia Scripts
is a trademark of
Dodo Books Indian Ocean Ltd. and OmniScriptum S.R.L publishing group

120 High Road, East Finchley, London, N2 9ED, United Kingdom
Str. Armeneasca 28/1, office 1, Chisinau MD-2012, Republic of Moldova, Europe
Managing Directors: Ieva Konstantinova, Victoria Ursu
info@omniscriptum.com

Printed at: see last page
ISBN: 978-620-8-38667-2

Credits

Jorge Octavio Guzmán Sánchez is a professor in the Computer Systems Engineering department of the Tecnológico Nacional de México / IT of Tuxtla Gutiérrez, and it is here where he taught the subject of "Advanced Web Development", it is thanks to this that for several years he was able to collect this knowledge that seeks to be in a text that can serve as teaching material for students taking the aforementioned subject.

Table of Contents

1.- Introduction

As I mentioned before, this is not a programming book, so we will not see concepts such as data types, variables, constants, control structures, even though this text talks about some languages such as PHP, for this reason it is not a book of object-oriented programming, but we will discuss the basic concepts of this paradigm as well as we will refer to several of these concepts.

For several years I have seen that there is no text that contains all (or most) of the topics of this subject (like others) and students resort to the internet, but find a lot of opinions (in this case also versions) without the advice that integrates all the concepts, the idea of this writing came up to demonstrate application of the topics in LARAVEL.

For example, they look for how to implement authentication in LARAVEL and they are told that it is very simple, as simple as running the command php artisan make:auth but they do not tell them that this worked in versions 5.x and was removed in version 6, in other sources of information they will find that they must add a package called ui but this worked in versions 6.x and lower than 8, and in others they will recommend you to use the jetstream package but they will hardly explain the steps to make it work and the bases that this has, for this reason I decided to make these notes in which I explain step by step how to perform the operations.

Object-oriented programming

For the Royal Academy of the Spanish language a paradigm is a theory or set of theories whose central core is accepted without question and that provides the basis and model for solving problems and advancing knowledge (among other meanings) but we will summarize it as "THE WAY OF THINKING", and a programming paradigm is how we think about the solution of a problem that we will then code.

In OOP what interests us are the objects involved in the process to be automated and that is why the first of the pillars (the first feature that we will see) is the **abstraction**: which is a mental process by which we only take the aspects that in our opinion are relevant to the problem we are working on and with these we declare the classes in the programming language used.

The next pillar of OOP is **encapsulation**, which is a strategy with which we can define how the features we abstracted earlier can be accessed and determine how they are used by other objects. First, we will identify the difference between class and object. The former is the statement: take the blueprint of a house as an example. The object, on the other hand, is the instance of a class; consider that every time a house is built in a subdivision, they are all based on the same blueprints.
There are three levels of encapsulation. The two extremes are easy to assimilate: **public** and **private**. In a class, attributes can be public or private to define the access that an object can have to them. For example, if we define the class "worker" and we establish that a characteristic of this is "salary", we can also establish that it is private, that is to say, that any other object will not be able to have direct access to this property since it only belongs to the instance itself, any other object will not be able to be granted access, to understand the following level (the protected one) it is necessary first to introduce the next pillar.

The next pillar is **inheritance**, this is a mechanism by which a class is allowed to be the basis for another(s) that will be the derivative(s). This is where the not-so-correct terms "parent class" and "child class" come in. As a result of this, the classes that inherit have the same characteristics of the class that was its base, here enters the third level of encapsulation that was not addressed before the **protected** understand how (private to others and public among the family).

Finally, there is the **polymorphism,** which is the ability to perform something in *several ways*, suppose we have a base class called animal and one of its methods is to express itself, and we create two classes, one is called dog and the other will be cat, both are classes derived from the animal class, both have a method that allows them to express themselves, but we can implement that they express themselves in different ways, the first will express itself by barking and the second by meowing.

They are known as PILLARS of object oriented programming because thanks to these strategies it is possible to code a complete program. As I said at the beginning "This is not a book of object oriented programming", we only want to make clear that these are necessary concepts to program with a framework since they are based on a language and the one we will work with is LARAVEL that uses PHP which is an object oriented language.

Design patterns

Since we are talking about programming issues we must remember the concept of design pattern since framworks use them, let's define this as "a way to solve a problem that is proven to work", this sentence is very generic, according to Gustavo Damian Campo who teaches at the Faculty of Engineering of the Catholic University of Salta, Argentina "A design pattern is a repeatable solution to a recurring problem in software design". [1]The most obvious one is perhaps the MVC (Model View Controller Pattern), which I personally associate with the phrase "divide and conquer".

The **model** is the part that contains the logic of the application, commonly it contains the access to the data used in the solution of the problem (it is here where the database is accessed), the **view** is the part that determines how this data is presented to the user and the **controller** is in charge of deciding how the system should react to the requests made by the end user.

There are different types of patterns, among them are the creative, structural and behavioral, examples of the first ones would be the *singleton* pattern or the *factory,* both explain how to create an object, the first one shows us how we can create an instance that will be shared throughout the application and that any object will use the same data. The next one allows us to create instances that will be used in different situations, but all from the same origin. There are structural patterns such as the *decorator* that show us how we can add new functionalities to an already declared "object". When we want to perform tasks that depend on each other, but in a decoupled way, we can use the *observer* pattern (which is considered a compartmental pattern).

And so there are many more.

Conventions

It is difficult to modify a source code when its content is not understood. In order that several people give the same meaning and implement their code in a similar way, there are conventions, remember that these are a form agreed upon by the majority to perform some activity, unlike a standard that must be respected.

All of us as programmers know that one must call variables *x, y or z* and possibly when we were taught this we were told to use variable names that expressed what they contained or what they were used for.

naming conventions.

In most programming languages the rule for creating identifiers is that they can begin with an underscore, and continue with one or more letters and or numbers, there are reserved words that depend on each dialect and these cannot be used, but in general it is not possible to use blanks.

The naming conventions are used to specify identifiers, and are **camelCase**, **PascalCase**, **snake_case**, **kebab-case**. In all of these the whitespace is substituted, the form is as follows.

In PascalCase and camelCase, capital letters are used at the beginning of each of the words that make up the name of the identifier, but in camelCase, capital letters are used from the second word onwards.

Snake_case is all lowercase and spaces are replaced by a hyphen sign.

The kebab-case convention is used to name identifiers other than element names used in an expression since the programming language would interpret it as a subtraction.

We are going to exemplify the use of each one of these conventions with the identifier "slow car", in **camel** case it would be written as carroLento; in **pascal** case it would be written as CarroLento, if it were named with snake case we would write carro_lento and finally the kebab case in this one would be named carro-lento.

Framework concept

This will be a book in which I will teach how to create an application using the LARAVEL framework, I emphasize once again that this is not a programming book; We have mentioned on multiple occasions the word framework, Marcelo Cíceri in his book Introduction to Laravel: Robust and Large Scale Applications defines it as "a set of predefined and interconnected software structures and components that serve as the basis for the organization and development of general purpose systems." [2] we will understand that a framework is an incomplete but functional application (its function typically is a "hello world") and the programmer must modify (add or remove certain parts or functionalities) to adapt the result to the client's requirements, so we can understand that a framework is a set of rules and conventions that are used in different areas of work to perform activities more efficiently and quickly. There are several types of frameworks for all the branches of knowledge, let's take into account that this is a kind of gioser[1] in which in a simple way the spaces are filled (not to draw letters and form a text, but to achieve an objective), if it is a marketing framework it is filled with the necessary actions to achieve the sale that is sought, if this is one of development the objective is to create a program of certain characteristics so the things that will be added will be libraries and code that facilitates to reach the established objective.

[1] A gioser is a thick paper stencil, which is used to trace letters.

As previously mentioned there are multiple types of frameworks, the ones we are interested in are those of development specifically web development, each one is based on a programming language, in the case of JAVA we have Spring, Struts and others, in the case of JAVASCRIPT we have Express and Nextjs and in the case of PHP we have Laravel, Symfony, Zend and others; All the previous lists are enunciative not limitative, in the same way there are frameworks that are known as **front end** and others are known as **back end**, these names allude to the part that these are executed, the first are at the end that the end customer sees (these are those that modify the views and example of these is angular, vue and others) and the others are executed on the server, there are times when the frameworks can be back or front, as is the case of LARAVEL and in this case they are known as **full stack**.

Development tools

Another topic to discuss will be the tools that we will use to create our development environment, first of all, is **COMPOSER**[2] , which is a dependency manager for PHP.

On several occasions you may have encountered a message that it is not possible to install software *x* because the software *y* is not installed on your computer (commonly happens if you want to install office and do not have the .Net framework), this will no longer happen because your application will have a configuration file called composer.json (this is the configuration file is in JavaScript Object Notation format), not to be confused with the composer.lock file, the former describes the packages that are required to install the application and the latter describes the packages that have been installed.

Another tool is **GIT**[3] which is a distributed version controller, this software allows you to keep track of the source code files that you develop, from time to time you make "commits" which are how snapshots to the code and these generate a unique identifier for each one (hash), at any time you can go back to a previous version (snapshot). The distributed feature is because several users can make modifications to the same project (repository).

Another tool is **NGROCK**[4] , it is a reverse proxy, that is to say that it is a software through which others can have access to the resources that you establish, if you are developing a system with the help of a web server then in port 80 of your machine you will be able to see the result, but other people will not be able to directly, they could configure their devices to be in the same network and they can see the system in their IP address, but with ngrock an address of the type http://fca2fa3fd170 will be generated.ngrok.io and all the requests that anyone makes through the internet will be redirected to the web application on your computer.

[2] It can be downloaded from their website https://getcomposer.org/

[3] You can download it at https://git-scm.com/downloads

[4] It can be found on their website https://ngrok.com/

Use of homestead

For Windows users whose computer does not work fluently with virtual machines it is recommended to use **LARAGON**[5] , this part of this writing is optional and can be omitted since you can also use a development environment with other tools like xamp, wamp, etc. When using **VAGRANT**[6] you do not depend on any specific hypervisor to manage the virtual machines (you can use virtualbox from oracle or vmware or other), with this it is possible to create your own development environment (later we will demonstrate its use).

The virtual machines install an operating system and for this ISO images are used, in the case of vagrant what is used are boxes (BOXes). The creators of the LARAVEL framework also created the BOX Homestead[7] , is an installation based on Ubuntu and has preloaded several tools that facilitate web development.

```yaml
Homestead.yaml...
---
ip: "192.168.10.10"
memory: 2048
cpus: 2
provider: virtualbox

authorize: ~/.ssh/id_rsa.pub

keys:
    - ~/.ssh/id_rsa

folders:
    - map: ~/code
      to: /home/vagrant/code

sites:
    - map: homestead.test
      to: /home/vagrant/code/public
    - map: prueba1.tst
      to: /home/vagrant/code/proyecto/public
      php: "7.4"
    - map: prueba2.local
      to: /home/vagrant/code/otro/public
      php: "8.0"

databases:
    - homestead

features:
    - mariadb: false
    - ohmyzsh: false
    - webdriver: false

#services:
#     - enabled:
#         - "postgresql@12-main"
#     - disabled:
#         - "postgresql@11-main"

# ports:
#     - send: 50000
#       to: 5000
#     - send: 7777
#       to: 777
#       protocol: udp
```

First, we need to clone (in git jargon we use the git clone command which makes a copy) the laravel/homestead repository from github. Following this we will modify the configuration file Homestead.yalm (when we download our copy we can base it on the Homestead.yalm.example) to define how we want the virtual machine we will use to be, set the IP, how much ram memory we will assign it, how many processors and if we want to share any folders from our host machine (physical machine) to our host (virtual machine) the above is declared in the folders section, in which you will find an entry called map which means that whatever we have in a certain location of our file system (the ~/code) means in the subdirectory code of the root directory of the current user (the user who is using vagrant), we must remember that the directory in which we start will be the one that contains our configuration file) and the entry to is the address of where this folder will be (if you have used linux maybe you are familiar with the term mount a file system), you have other sections how the sites, which specifies the sites that will have our virtual machine, this environment has preconfigured nginx[8] with support for multiple hosts, each one of them is configured according to the sites entries, to each one of these you can specify an attribute called php, this is used to establish the version of this language that will have this site, you must remember that homstead depending on the version has installed multiple tools and also several versions of php, so it is possible to declare that in test1.test use php in version 7.4 and in test2.test use php in version 8 (the names of the sites are established with the entry map and the location of the files that will have this site are established with the entry to) there are several more sections but by configuring these you can create your development environment.

[5] A bundle that installs together with a web server the necessary tools for the development of LARAVEL projects.

[6] VAGRANT is a virtual machine manager.

[7] You can read at https://laravel.com/docs/9.x/homestead

[8] A high-performance web server that can also be configured as a reverse proxy.

To start the virtual machine we use the command vagrant up and to shut it down we will use the vagrant halt, every time we make a change in the configuration we will use the vagrant reload -provision, it is important to use the provision modifier otherwise it would be like "restarting the machine, but not reloading the configuration that we modified.

2.- First steps with LARAVEL

First we will install the framework, to perform this action there are several ways, we will start by using the composer tool (which as we saw before is a dependency manager) that will read the composer.json file and in it are the requirements to install the application (remember that the composer.lock file contains the versions of the requirements that were already installed), if we review the content of the composer.json file we find that it is required to have PHP version 8.0.2 or higher as well as 9.19 or higher of the framework and other specifications.

```
pruebas@otro:~/ejercicio$ cat composer.json
{
    "name": "laravel/laravel",
    "type": "project",
    "description": "The Laravel Framework.",
    "keywords": ["framework", "laravel"],
    "license": "MIT",
    "require": {
        "php": "^8.0.2",
        "guzzlehttp/guzzle": "^7.2",
        "laravel/framework": "^9.19",
        "laravel/sanctum": "^3.0",
        "laravel/tinker": "^2.7"
    },
    "require-dev": {
        "fakerphp/faker": "^1.9.1",
        "laravel/pint": "^1.0",
        "laravel/sail": "^1.0.1",
        "mockery/mockery": "^1.4.4",
        "nunomaduro/collision": "^6.1",
        "phpunit/phpunit": "^9.5.10",
        "spatie/laravel-ignition": "^1.0"
    },
    "autoload": {
        "psr-4": {
            "App\\": "app/",
            "Database\\Factories\\": "database/factories/",
            "Database\\Seeders\\": "database/seeders/"
        }
    },
    "autoload-dev": {
        "psr-4": {
            "Tests\\": "tests/"
        }
    },
    "scripts": {
        "post-autoload-dump": [
            "Illuminate\\Foundation\\ComposerScripts::postAutoloadDump",
            "@php artisan package:discover --ansi"
        ],
        "post-update-cmd": [
            "@php artisan vendor:publish --tag=laravel-assets --ansi --force"
        ],
        "post-root-package-install": [
            "@php -r \"file_exists('.env') || copy('.env.example', '.env');\""
        ],
        "post-create-project-cmd": [
            "@php artisan key:generate --ansi"
        ]
    },
    "extra": {
        "laravel": {
            "dont-discover": []
        }
    },
    "config": {
        "optimize-autoloader": true,
        "preferred-install": "dist",
        "sort-packages": true,
        "allow-plugins": {
            "pestphp/pest-plugin": true
        }
    },
    "minimum-stability": "dev",
    "prefer-stable": true
}
pruebas@otro:~/ejercicio$
```

When we use the tool it checks if the dependency that is indicated was already downloaded previously and is in cache and installs it otherwise it downloads it to install it, with it we can also create a project, even tell it in which version we want:

```
pruebas@otro:~$ composer create-project laravel/laravel="5.1.*" ejercicio
Creating a "laravel/laravel=5.1.*" project at "./ejercicio"
Installing laravel/laravel (v5.1.33)
  - Installing laravel/laravel (v5.1.33): Extracting archive
Created project in /home/pruebas/ejercicio
> php -r "copy('.env.example', '.env');"
Loading composer repositories with package information
Updating dependencies
Lock file operations: 58 installs, 0 updates, 0 removals
  - Locking classpreloader/classpreloader (3.2.1)
  - Locking danielstjules/stringy (1.10.0)
  - Locking dnoegel/php-xdg-base-dir (0.1)
  - Locking doctrine/inflector (1.4.4)
  - Locking doctrine/instantiator (1.4.1)
  - Locking fzaninotto/faker (v1.5.0)
  - Locking hamcrest/hamcrest-php (v1.2.2)
  - Locking jakub-onderka/php-console-color (v0.2)
  - Locking jakub-onderka/php-console-highlighter (v0.3.2)
```

In the previous example it was indicated to create a project based on the laravel/laravel repository (as we said before it is user/repository) and that we want version 5.1. (this was only for demonstration and it is not the best since this version is already obsolete, that is why if we do not specify one we install the current one (which at the time of this writing is 9.3.9).

```
pruebas@otro:~$ composer create-project laravel/laravel ejercicio
Creating a "laravel/laravel" project at "./ejercicio"
Installing laravel/laravel (v9.3.9)
  - Installing laravel/laravel (v9.3.9): Extracting archive
Created project in /home/pruebas/ejercicio
> @php -r "file_exists('.env') || copy('.env.example', '.env');"
Loading composer repositories with package information
Updating dependencies
Lock file operations: 107 installs, 0 updates, 0 removals
  - Locking brick/math (0.10.2)
  - Locking dflydev/dot-access-data (v3.0.1)
  - Locking doctrine/inflector (2.0.6)
  - Locking doctrine/instantiator (1.4.1)
  - Locking doctrine/lexer (1.2.3)
  - Locking dragonmantank/cron-expression (v3.3.2)
  - Locking egulias/email-validator (3.2.1)
  - Locking fakerphp/faker (v1.20.0)
  - Locking filp/whoops (2.14.5)
```

But there is an installer that was developed by the creators of the framework, we install it with the command:

```
pruebas@otro:~$ composer create-project laravel/installer
Creating a "laravel/installer" project at "./installer"
Installing laravel/installer (v4.2.17)
  - Installing laravel/installer (v4.2.17): Extracting archive
Created project in /home/pruebas/installer
Loading composer repositories with package information
Updating dependencies
Lock file operations: 37 installs, 0 updates, 0 removals
  - Locking doctrine/instantiator (1.4.1)
  - Locking myclabs/deep-copy (1.11.0)
  - Locking nikic/php-parser (v4.15.1)
  - Locking phar-io/manifest (2.0.3)
  - Locking phar-io/version (3.2.1)
  - Locking phpunit/php-code-coverage (9.2.17)
  - Locking phpunit/php-file-iterator (3.0.6)
  - Locking phpunit/php-invoker (3.1.1)
  - Locking phpunit/php-text-template (2.0.4)
  - Locking phpunit/php-timer (5.0.3)
```

As a name for the folder was not specified at the end, it will create a folder called installer.

```
pruebas@otro:~$ ls
installer
pruebas@otro:~$ ls installer/
bin  composer.json  composer.lock  LICENSE.md  README.md  src  vendor
pruebas@otro:~$ ls installer/bin/
laravel
pruebas@otro:~$ 
```

Inside the installer you will find the installer in the bin folder and using it you can create a new project containing the framework

```
pruebas@otro:~$ ./installer/bin/laravel new ejercicio

 _                               _
| |                             | |
| |     __ _ _ __ __ ___   _____| |
| |    / _` | '__/ _` \ \ / / _ \ |
| |___| (_| | | | (_| |\ V /  __/ |
|______\__,_|_|  \__,_| \_/ \___|_|

Creating a "laravel/laravel" project at "./ejercicio"
Info from https://repo.packagist.org: #StandWithUkraine
Installing laravel/laravel (v9.3.9)
  - Installing laravel/laravel (v9.3.9): Extracting archive
Created project in /home/pruebas/ejercicio
> @php -r "file_exists('.env') || copy('.env.example', '.env');"
Loading composer repositories with package information
Updating dependencies
Lock file operations: 107 installs, 0 updates, 0 removals
  - Locking brick/math (0.10.2)
  - Locking dflydev/dot-access-data (v3.0.1)
  - Locking doctrine/inflector (2.0.6)
  - Locking doctrine/instantiator (1.4.1)
  - Locking doctrine/lexer (1.2.3)
```

But we can also install it step by step; for this we will clone it using git (if we do not specify the name of a folder at the end of the command it will leave the project in a folder named like the repository).

```
pruebas@otro:~$ git clone https://github.com/laravel/laravel.git ejercicio
Cloning into 'ejercicio'...
remote: Enumerating objects: 33557, done.
remote: Counting objects: 100% (1/1), done.
remote: Total 33557 (delta 0), reused 0 (delta 0), pack-reused 33556
Receiving objects: 100% (33557/33557), 10.25 MiB | 3.47 MiB/s, done.
Resolving deltas: 100% (19855/19855), done.
```

The exercise directory contains the framework, but we still lack several details to use it, first we must create a general configuration file for the framework, this is the .env file and for this we can be guided by the .env.example file (in unix based operating systems the files whose names begin with a dot are hidden).

We will make a copy of the **.env.example** file (remember that it must be in the exercise folder, you can do it from a file explorer as well. There are also those who rename the example file.

It is time to install the dependencies, for this we will make use of the composer tool, we can see the composer.json file that is among the files that were downloaded, if you review it you will find that it states how required the laravel/framework package (we already commented that it is based on github and it is read as user/repository)

```
pruebas@otro:~/ejercicio$ cat composer.json
{
    "name": "laravel/laravel",
    "type": "project",
    "description": "The Laravel Framework.",
    "keywords": ["framework", "laravel"],
    "license": "MIT",
    "require": {
        "php": "^8.0.2",
        "guzzlehttp/guzzle": "^7.2",
        "laravel/framework": "^9.19",
        "laravel/sanctum": "^3.0",
        "laravel/tinker": "^2.7"
    },
```

the command we will use to check if we have the requirements installed is update

```
pruebas@otro:~/ejercicio$ composer  update
Loading composer repositories with package information
Updating dependencies
Lock file operations: 107 installs, 0 updates, 0 removals
  - Locking brick/math (0.10.2)
  - Locking dflydev/dot-access-data (v3.0.1)
  - Locking doctrine/inflector (2.0.6)
  - Locking doctrine/instantiator (1.4.1)
  - Locking doctrine/lexer (1.2.3)
  - Locking dragonmantank/cron-expression (v3.3.2)
  - Locking egulias/email-validator (3.2.1)
  - Locking fakerphp/faker (v1.20.0)
  - Locking filp/whoops (2.14.5)
  - Locking fruitcake/php-cors (v1.2.0)
  - Locking graham-campbell/result-type (v1.1.0)
  - Locking guzzlehttp/guzzle (7.5.0)
  - Locking guzzlehttp/promises (1.5.2)
  - Locking guzzlehttp/psr7 (2.4.1)
  - Locking hamcrest/hamcrest-php (v2.0.1)
  - Locking laravel/framework (v9.36.4)
  - Locking laravel/pint (v1.2.0)
  - Locking laravel/sail (v1.16.2)
  - Locking laravel/sanctum (v3.0.1)
  - Locking laravel/serializable-closure (v1.2.2)
  - Locking laravel/tinker (v2.7.2)
  - Locking league/commonmark (2.3.5)
  - Locking league/config (v1.1.1)
  - Locking league/flysystem (3.10.1)
  - Locking league/mime-type-detection (1.11.0)
  - Locking mockery/mockery (1.5.1)
  - Locking monolog/monolog (2.8.0)
  - Locking myclabs/deep-copy (1.11.0)
```

Laravel handles for security a token based on an encryption key so now we will use the artisan script of the framework, to generate this key, being in the root of the project we run the following command

```
pruebas@otro:~/ejercicio$ php artisan key:generate

  INFO  Application key set successfully.

pruebas@otro:~/ejercicio$ cat .env
APP_NAME=Laravel
APP_ENV=local
APP_KEY=base64:Pz5e5NDOqGY2vEw2PFitpFj702SKraO2PEobVEC6hjY=
APP_DEBUG=true
APP_URL=http://localhost
```

I was able to confirm that the APP_KEY variable in the .env file has changed from a clean string to a string in base 64

We will explain the previous command, first of all, we call the PHP interpreter since artisan is a script in this language and it is the main one with which we can create elements, perform actions, etc... in other words, use the LARAVEL framework.

The parameter key is the command and after the colon we indicate the subcommand, in this case we are generating the key (key does not have a variety of subcommands like others, for example make).

Now that we have configured (the basics needed) we can see the framework in action, for this we will use the serve command (what this does is to run a development web server), it installs it on port 8000 unlike a web server is usually on port 80.

```
pruebas@otro:~/ejercicio$ php artisan serve

  INFO  Server running on [http://127.0.0.1:8000].

  Press Ctrl+C to stop the server
```

We can change the ip (it could be the one you want your machine to use on the intranet) and we can change the port as well.

```
pruebas@otro:~/ejercicio$ php artisan serve --host=192.168.56.106 --port=8081

  INFO  Server running on [http://192.168.56.106:8081].

  Press Ctrl+C to stop the server
```

y

now we will be able to see our system from a web browser (even from another machine if we don't have a firewall activated).

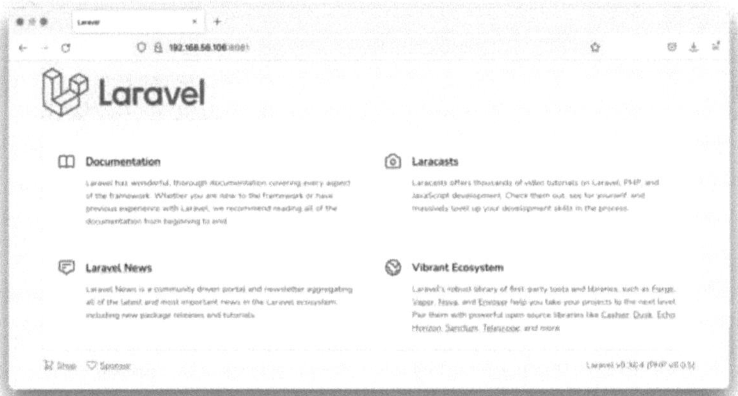

Note, when we created the exercise (either with the installer or with the composer tool) we ran all the steps, installed dependencies, generated the .env file and added the encryption key.

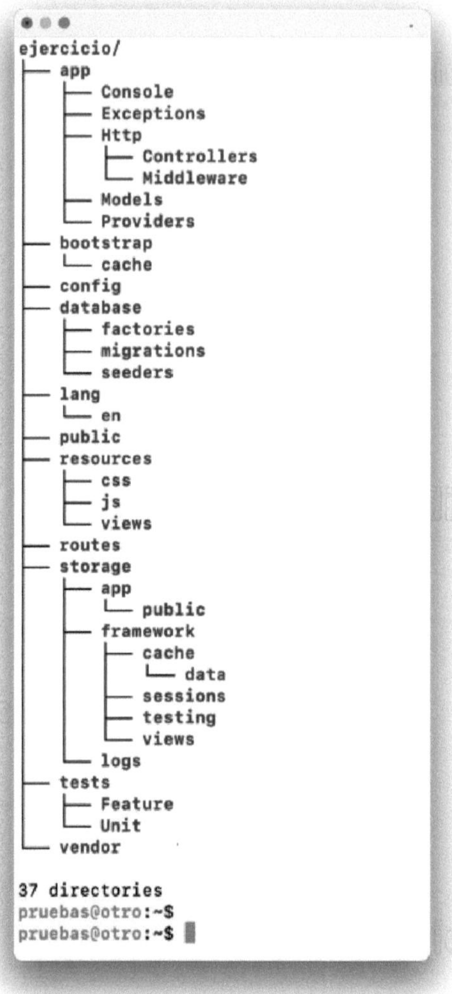

It is time to know the folders and files of the framework, for this we will explore the frameworkr (in different versions you may or may not find some of these, but we show the most relevant)

We will start by explaining the directories of the framework, then we will explain the important files

Firstly, we have the **app** directory, we can say that the application (or most of it) will be inside this directory, it is here where we have a directory for commands that are executed from the console, these are the ones that we can execute with the artisan script, LARAVEL already brings several, we can create our own. Next, we will find the **Exceptions** directory, in it we will put the code that we want to be executed when an exception is found (as in several languages we use the *try-catch*, we can define the logic with which we will treat that error and we can also define how the system will look like.

We have the **Http** folder, which contains the **Controllers** and **Middlware** folders (and others that will be created as needed), the first one will contain the controllers (which are the classes that define the behavior that the system will have before certain requests, and the second one is the folder where the filters to the requests will be stored, in them we can determine what the system will do before a certain request, It is here where we can validate if the request has certain conditions, for example if the request is from a certain address or meets certain criteria, not to be confused with the **FormRequest** that are classes that can validate the input fields that normally come from a form, for example validate that a data is numeric, or required, etcetera.)

We continue inside the **app** folder with the **Models** folder (ignoring the User.php model that by default already exists in the installation) here the models generated for our systems are saved, commonly the models are the ones that are in charge of saving the data used in our application in the case of LARAVEL these work with the database through eloquent (ORM[9]) used by the framework. In previous versions there was no special folder to store them.

Finally we find a folder to store the **Providers**, the installation already has some classes, these providers are responsible for configuring and loading some aspects of the application, we commonly say that in the app folder is the system (or at least most of it) because as we create events, emails and other aspects the code that is generated will be in sub folders of this (most of the classes that are created). The next folder to analyze is bootstrap (this is a folder of the framework for the initialization of the application, not to be confused with the css bootstrap).

The next folder is the configuration folder, it is called **config** and inside it we will find php files (classes that return arrays with the configuration that certain parts of the system must have).

We have arrived to the **database** folder, in it we can find the database configurations, we find three sub folders, the first one we will analyze is **migrations** since it is here where we define each of the components of the database, the next one is **seeders** which is where we feed the data of our database (this is a mechanism to create for example a "default" user or if for example we were developing a system of car parts it would be necessary to have a catalog with the brands of the cars, and it is here that we could feed this table) and finally we will analyze the **factories folder**, it is through these that we can populate our database with records for testing, generally this is also done with **seeders** since it is here that we could feed this table, and it is here that we could feed this table) and finally we will analyze the **factories** folder, it is through these that we can populate our database with records for testing, generally we also do this with seeders since usually the factories generate random data.

We continue with the **lang** folder that has a sub folder **in**, this is to handle multiple languages for the application, by default the application works in the English language but this can be changed in the configuration (app.php file located in the config directory), on the internet you will find open source projects to change the language of the application, ie add a sub folder.

It is time to check the **public** folder which is the starting point of our application, if you put any file inside it it will be available to anyone through the network, the web server defines this as the home folder.

The resources folder as its name indicates contains the resources used by the application, it contains three sub folders, the first one that we will analyze is views and in it as its name indicates we will include the pages that will be the "view" of our application, these

[9] Object Relational Mapping, is a way of programming in which all the elements of the database are mapped to object oriented programming, later we will discuss this topic in detail.

will be rendered as html in the web browser of who uses our system; the other two folders (js and css) are used by a "preprocessor" currently LARAVEL uses VITE to generate the files app.js and app.css files with the resources that our application uses and places them in the public folder (in previous versions it used webpack, but we can not use it and include our "assets" directly).

The next folder is **routes**, this directory contains the files api.php, channels.php, console.php and web.php, and in them we will define how the system will react to the requests that a user makes. It is possible to define in the file in which the routes will be searched depending on the type of application that is handled, for example if it is a web application when the user enters the URL http://servidor/amigos/listar the route is searched in the web.php file that is inside this folder and in this we can define the action to be carried out).

In the list the following directory is **storage**, and its functionality is to save, but it depends on the sub folder use, the ones you have are app, framework, and logs, the contents of the **framework** folder (and its sub directories) are files that LARAVEL uses, for example the views compiled in php, the session files that are managed, etc.., the **logs** folder contains the log files that the system generates, by defeto there is a file called laravel.log in which the errors that are generated are registered, and we have the **app** folder in which we save files that are stored in our application, for example files with photos that we can upload.

The **tests** folder contains two sub folders **Feature** and **Unit**, it is here where we can save the files that define our tests that will be performed on the system, whether they are functionality tests or unit tests.

And now we have the **vendor** folder in which we do not really save files, this is the folder in which the libraries that are necessary to run the application are saved, remember that the composer tool downloads all the requirements and if you modify any file that is inside the vendor the next time composer updates it will download new files and overwrite the changes.

When we talk about the special files that are in the root of the project we will find the files: composer.json, composer.lock, package.json, phpunit.xml, README.md and vite.config.js, of the first two we had already explained, the third one is to npm[10] as the first one to the composer tool, we also have the case of an xml file in which the testing system of the framework is configured, the penultimate one as its name suggests has information about the project and the last one is the configuration that allows to complete the assets (java script and css resources that will be included in the project, after the compilation with vite (in previous versions of laravel we used webpack) this is not necessary since the files app.css and app.js files that are generated with the compilation and located in public can be replaced by libraries or cdn's to these.

It is time to talk more in depth about the routes, the examples will be given with the web routes (but similarly to a web application can create routes for an API or others that LARAVEL handles).

[10] Acronimo de node pakage manager, a node package manager (which is based on java script)

In the /routes/web.php file, the ROUTE facade is included by default.

```
use Illuminate "Support for the routing;
```

with this instruction we are saying that in the code of this file we can use the ROUTE class that is defined in this address (if we are observers we are making reference to a file located in the vendor folder specifically /laravel/framework/src/Illuminate/Support/Facades/Route.php and if we observe it is part of the framework, this class allows us to define new routes, that is to say when a user writes in the web client an "address" (that is to say a URL[11]) the actions that will be carried out, for this it is important to know what the **http verbs** are (in this writing we will only mention GET, PUT, POST and DELETE even though there are many others).

For example, we declare this route

```
Route::get('greet',function(){
   echo "HELLO";
});
```

That is indicating with an anonymous function that when the system receives a GET request that matches the URI "hello", it should print the word hello.

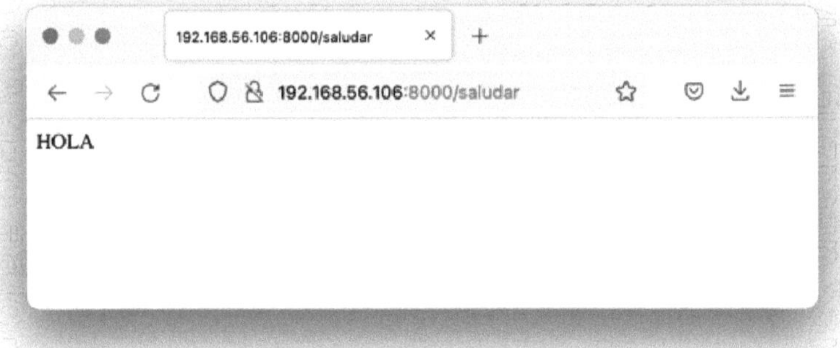

This way we could receive by parameter the name of the person we are going to greet.

```
Route::get('greet/{name}',function($parameter){
   $name = $parameter;
   echo "HELLO ";
   echo strtoupper($name);

});
```

[11] Uniform Resource Locator commonly known as web address, is the one we see in the address bar of the browser.

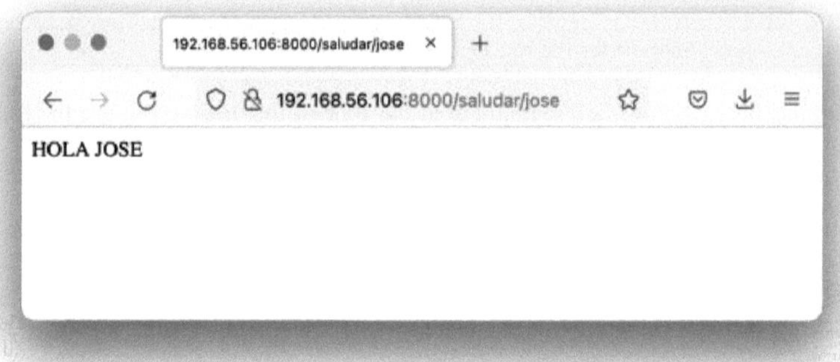

We can also pass another parameter that is the language in which we want to greet (English, French, Spanish).

```
Route::get('greet/{name}/{language}',function($parameter01, $parameter02){
   $name = $parameter01;
   $language = $parameter02;
   switch ($language) {
      case 'English':
         echo "HI ";
         echo strtoupper($name);
         break;
      case 'French':
         echo "SALUT ";
         echo strtoupper($name);
         break;
      case 'German':
         echo "HALLO ";
         echo strtoupper($name);
         break;
      default:
         echo "YOU HAVE NOT SPECIFIED ANY LANGUAGE";
         break;
   }
});
```

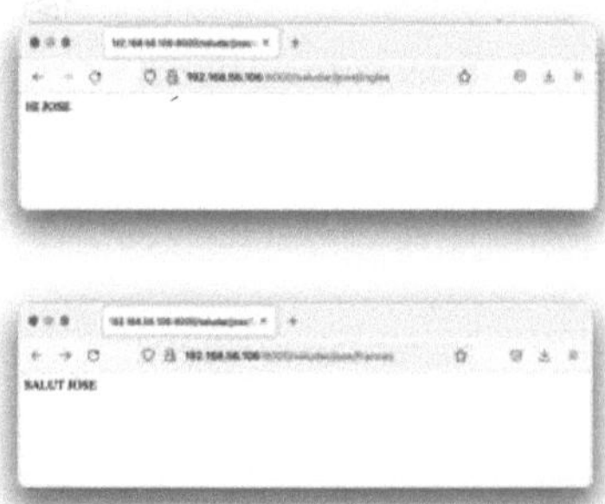

But if we do not enter the language, the system gives an error message, this is because we remember that in the definition of the route we stated that the second parameter was not optional.

We solve this by defining the second parameter as optional, and we will give the variable a default value

```
Route::get('greetings/{name}/{language?}',function($parameter01,
$parameter02='english'){
   $name = $parameter01;
   $language = $parameter02;
   switch ($language) {
      case 'English':
         echo "HI ";
         echo strtoupper($name);
         break;
      case 'French':
         echo "SALUT ";
         echo strtoupper($name);
         break;
      case 'German':
         echo "HALLO ";
         echo strtoupper($name);
         break;
      case 'Spanish':
         echo "HELLO ";
         echo strtoupper($name);
         break;
   }
});
```

So far we have solved everything from our web.php file but our system will continue to grow, we will add the functionality to ask for username and password, based on these credentials welcome the user or indicate that something was wrong, for this we will make a controller, these are used to group functionality as in the example we will see and can arise from two sources, a use case or the management of a model.

Partially the use case for logging in is:

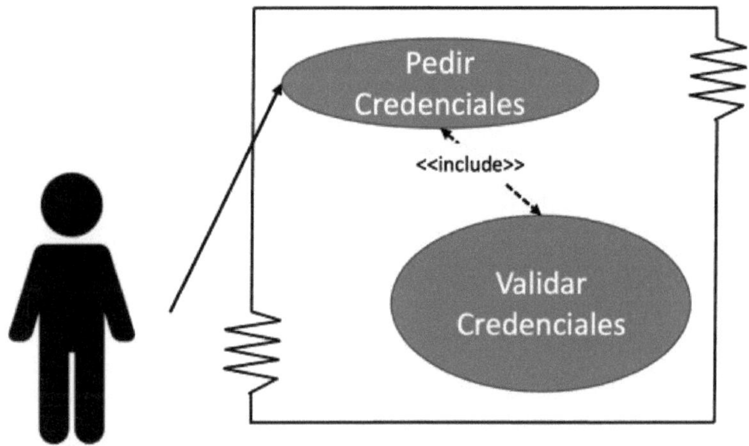

So we will create the controller called EntrarController (convention says that the name will be in PascalCase and end with the word Controller) so we will use the command :

```
php artisan make:controller LoginController
```

that generates the file EntrarController.php that contains the class EntrarController and is in the folder **Controllers** that is a sub folder of **Http** that is in **app**, in this class we will create the methods pedirCredenciales, validarCredenciales and salir (all these will be named using camel case[12]) and in these methods we will include the code that generates the desired functionality. In this way our web.php file will only have the reference of the method that we want to execute when a route is fulfilled.

Instead of using several lines of code (how it is done in lines 21 to 40 which was the greeting path we used in previous examples) we use a few lines for the paths in lines 51 and 52 but we will add features to these later (we created the product and dashboard paths only as a test).

[12] Notation style in which the first letter of each word is written in upper case (everything else in lower case) to avoid using spaces, but unlike pascalcase the first letter of the result will be lower case.

```
20  Route::get('saludar/{nombre}/{idioma?}',function($parametro01, $parametro02='español'){
21      $nombre = $parametro01;
22      $idioma = $parametro02;
23      switch ($idioma) {
24          case 'ingles':
25              echo "HI ";
26              echo strtoupper($nombre);
27              break;
28          case 'frances':
29              echo "SALUT ";
30              echo strtoupper($nombre);
31              break;
32          case 'aleman':
33              echo "HALLO ";
34              echo strtoupper($nombre);
35              break;
36          case 'español':
37              echo "HOLA ";
38              echo strtoupper($nombre);
39              break;
40      }
41  });
42
43  Route::get('dashboard', function () {
44      echo "dashoard del administrador";
45  });
46
47  Route::get('productos', function () {
48      echo "mostar productos al cliente";
49  });
50
51  Route::get('entrar',[\App\Http\Controllers\EntrarController::class,'pedirCredenciales']);
52  Route::post('entrar',[\App\Http\Controllers\EntrarController::class,'validarCredenciales']);
53
```

We can optimize lines 51 and 52 by including the driver at the beginning of the web.php file with a

```
1   <?php
2
3   use Illuminate\Support\Facades\Route;
4   use App\Http\Controllers\EntrarController;
5
```

```
48  Route::get('productos', function () {
49      echo "mostar productos al cliente";
50  });
51  Route::get('entrar',[EntrarController::class,'pedirCredenciales']);
52  Route::post('entrar',[EntrarController::class,'validarCredenciales']);
53
```

Something that we must comment is that in LARAVEL from version 8 the namespace of the routes that the system used by default was eliminated, in previous versions we could define the route of line 51 as follows

```
Route::get('enter','EnterController@requestCredentials');
```

And in version 8 it would be

```
Route::get('log in','App\HttpControllers','App\HttpControllers'Log inController');
```

What is currently growing in code is the controller, which we will explain:

```
1   <?php
2
3   namespace App\Http\Controllers;
4
5   use Illuminate\Http\Request;
6
7   class EntrarController extends Controller
8   {
9       function pedirCredenciales(){
10          echo "<html><head><title>ENTRADA</title></head><body>";
11          echo "<form method='post'>usuario:<input type='text' name='usr'><br>";
12          echo "clave:<input type='password' name='pwd'><br>";
13          echo "<input type='submit' value='enviar'></form></body></html>";
14      }
15      function validarCredenciales(Request $request){
16          $usuario = $request->input('usr');
17          $password = $request->input('pwd');
18          // Revisar si el usuario introdujo la clave correcta.
19          if ($usuario == 'admin' && $password == 'nimda')
20              return redirect('dashboard');
21          if ($usuario == 'cliente' && $password == 'etneilc')
22              return redirect('productos');
23          return redirect()->back();
24      }
25  }
26
```

What we have added is from line 9 to 24, the rest was generated by the command make:controller

In line 9 we create the method requestCredentials that with several calls to the function echo of php we print a web page with a form that captures the user name (in a text box called usr and the password in a text box of type password that is called pwd), to the form we have assigned the POST method (remember what you know about the http verbs) as we have not assigned attribute acction the destination of the data acquired here will be the same path.

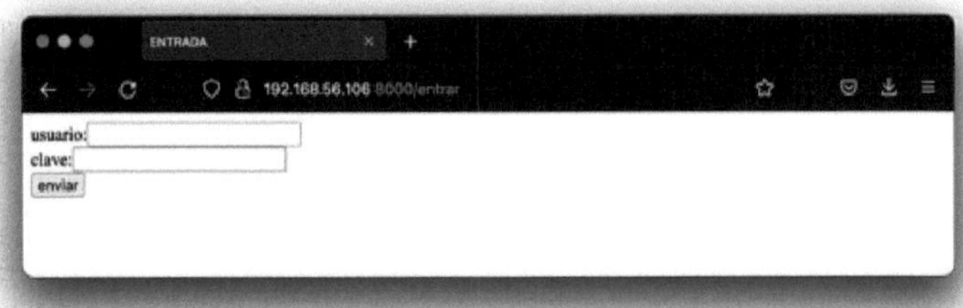

At this point, in order for the POST data sending to work, we must comment out the use of the middleware VerifyCsrfToken in the web key of the middlewareGroups array of the app/Http/Kernel.php file.

```
28         *
29         * @var array<string, array<int, class-string|string>>
30         */
31        protected $middlewareGroups = [
32            'web' => [
33                \App\Http\Middleware\EncryptCookies::class,
34                \Illuminate\Cookie\Middleware\AddQueuedCookiesToResponse::class,
35                \Illuminate\Session\Middleware\StartSession::class,
36                \Illuminate\View\Middleware\ShareErrorsFromSession::class,
37                //\App\Http\Middleware\VerifyCsrfToken::class,
38                \Illuminate\Routing\Middleware\SubstituteBindings::class,
39            ],
40
41            'api' => [
42                // \Laravel\Sanctum\Http\Middleware\EnsureFrontendRequestsAreStateful::class,
43                'throttle:api',
44                \Illuminate\Routing\Middleware\SubstituteBindings::class,
45            ],
46        ];
47
```

We will do this to make the example work for the moment, then we will remove this comment that we have included in line 37 (and later we will explain the use of middlewares by name if you have doubts you can investigate the csrf attack and this is a strategy that LARAVEL implements to avoid it).

It is time to explain the method validarCredenciales that begins in line 15 of our file EntrarController, we can observe that in the signature of the method we find that it receives as parameter the request (the request that the client sends to the server)[13] current, with this we can identify the origin of the request, as well as the variables that come in it. Then in line 16 we will obtain what the user wrote in the text box called usr (similar to what is done in the code that follows, but now it does it with the input pwd), the logic that we use for validation is extremely simple, if the user that was introduced is called **admin** and with password **nimda** we allow him to see the dashboard of the application, in a similar way if the user is called **client** and his password is the word **etneilc** he will be able to see the page of products, for that reason we use the function redirect and to this we pass him how parameter the route to which we want the system is directed. But if the credentials that were entered are not correct then the system will be redirected to the previous step (remember that before we were in the input form).

But we have not finished yet, it turns out that although now we have a web.php file that is understandable everything we have piled up in the controller and it is time to use the views. For this there is no command make:view, they are files that we create and can be scripts in php or blade (the latter is the template system that includes LARAVEL), has a special directory in which they are saved and this is called **views** which is located in the **resources** folder of our project.

We can say that Blade is like php to HTML, although the second one allows the use of variables and control structures (among other features) and the first one also adds other peculiarities, for example, data sanitization (it uses the php htmlspecialchars function to prevent an xss attack, if you want to print a variable as it comes you can use `{!! $variable !!}`), as well as other directives (in the cycles you have access to the `$loop` variable that gives you information of the iterations) and other more features.

[13] Let's remember that a client and a web server communicate using the http, and in a simplified way we will say that the client sends requests (some request) and receives what would be a response that is identified with a status code.

At this point we can define the view called pedir (actually is to create a php file called pedir.php that later we will convert into pedir.blade.php) that is inside the folder views, in this file we will write what would be an html page that asks for the two fields, in fact the old content of the method pedirCredenciales since this now will only return the instruction to load this view.

```
function requestCredentials(){
    return view('request');
}
```

```
<!DOCTYPE html>
<html lang="es">
<head>
    <meta charset="UTF-8">
    <meta http-equiv="X-UA-Compatible" content="IE=edge">
    <meta name="viewport" content="width=device-width, initial-scale=1.0">
    <title>Document</title>
</head>
<body>
    <form method="post">
        usuario: <input type="text" name="usr"><br>
        clave: <input type="password" name="pwd"><br>
        <input type='submit' value='enviar'>
    </form>
</body>
</html>
```

Illustration 1 Code of the file request.php

The behavior of the system remains the same, but we have managed to separate the elements of the program, so that it complies with the saying "cobbler to your shoes", now we can assign the views to a designer (or someone who specializes in UX/UI) and it is another person who works on the programming (the validation code).

But the features that the framework offers us are many and we are just getting to know them, as I mentioned before there is blade, and we can define that this is what php is to html, and therefore instead of the file request has the extension php now it will be a file ".blade.php" (there is precedence if there are several files that are called the same but have different extensions one is html, another php and another is blade.php then the view function will load the last file type before the second and before the third.php then the view function will load the last type of file before the second and before the third), if we want to pass some variable to the view that we define we can do this in several ways, one of them is to use the compact function of php and then assign it as a parameter to the view.

Now our method would look like this:

```
function requestCredentials(){
    $system = "EXAMPLE";
    return view('request', compact('system'));
}
```

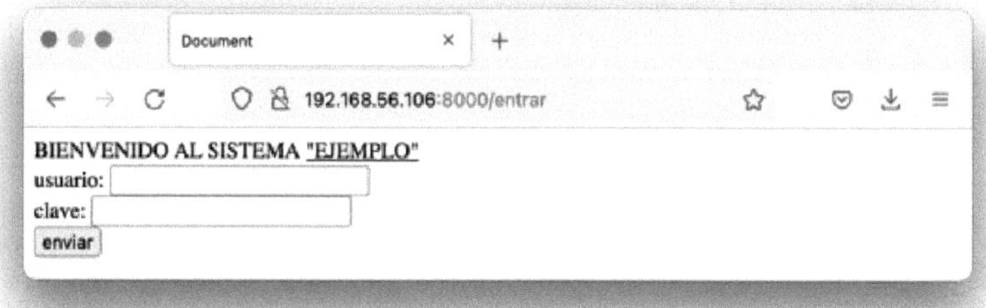

And the view looked like this:

```
<!DOCTYPE html>
<html lang="es">
<head>
    <meta charset="UTF-8">
    <meta http-equiv="X-UA-Compatible" content="IE=edge">
    <meta name="viewport" content="width=device-width, initial-scale=1.0">
    <title>Document</title>
</head>
<body>
    BIENVENIDO AL SISTEMA <u>"{{$sistema}}"</u>
    <form method="post">
        usuario: <input type="text" name="usr"><br>
        clave: <input type="password" name="pwd"><br>
        <input type='submit' value='enviar'>
    </form>
</body>
</html>
```

Another aspect we will see will be the models, LARAVEL uses eloquent so if we run the command **php artisan make:model Conocido** the file Conocido.php is generated in the sub directory Models of the app folder (the convention marks that the names of the models will be in pascal case and singular, they really mention the entity).

But as we will not use databases yet we do not need neither to inherit from Model nor to use the trait[14] HasFactory so we can eliminate the references to these classes and instead we will put:

[14] A php strategy to allow multiple inheritance similar to the implementation of an interface, gives an attribute or method the possibility to be executed in the class context not in the instance context, i.e. it allows changes to be made but at a generic level, not a specific one.

Normally the models are in charge of saving in the database, everything that we require for the development of the application, as we still will not make use of the database to save in a semi persistent storage we will use a session (which is a file that exists in the server while we remain with an active connection using the system.

```php
<?php
namespace App\Models;

class Conocido{
    public $id;
    public $nombre;
    static public function all(){
        return session('datos',[ ]);
    }
    public function save(){
        $datos = session('datos',[]);
        $datos[$this->id]=$this->nombre;
        session(['datos' => $datos]);
        return true;
    }
    static public function  find($id){
        $datos = session('datos',[]);
        if(isset($datos[$id])){
            $nuevo = new Conocido();
            $nuevo->id = $id;
            $nuevo->nombre = $datos[$id];
            return $nuevo;
        }else{
            return null;
        }
    }
    static public function delete($id){
        $datos = session('datos',[]);
        unset($datos[$id]);
        session(['datos' => $datos]);
    }
}
```

We are defining the known class that will contain two attributes, one for the identifier and another for the name. We create several methods, the first one that is static (that is to say that this method belongs to the class itself not to the instance so it is possible to use it without having an object of this type), this method what it does is to take the variable that is called data that is in the session file and if there is nothing then it will return an empty array.

We have the **save** function which is an instance method, that is to say that it works with the data that are in the active copy, what it does is that the current data of the known with whom it is working will be saved in the session array, for this first all the data that are saved are taken, the element of the array that is currently working with the value in memory is updated and once the array is updated it is saved again in the session.

The next function that we will analyze is **find**, this is also static and what it does is that it receives by parameter the identifier of the resource with which we want to work to return a null value when it is not found or return an object containing the data retrieved from the session. Finally we have a static function and it is called delete, it receives the identifier of the resource on which we want to act, and deletes it.
The previous implementation is just to introduce the concept of model and to interact with it in our code we will use the class, to test it we will use a tool included with laravel, this is Tinker (a command line that interprets php code and has access to the project files), to use it the command we will use is

```
php artisan tinker
```

```
Psy Shell v0.11.8 (PHP 8.0.5 — cli) by Justin Hileman
>>> Conocido::all()
[!] Aliasing 'Conocido' to 'App\Models\Conocido' for this Tinker session.
=> []

>>> $nuevo = new Conocido()
=> App\Models\Conocido {#4587
     +id: null,
     +nombre: null,
   }

>>> $nuevo->id = 1
=> 1

>>> $nuevo->nombre = "Juan"
=> "Juan"

>>> $nuevo->save()
=> true

>>> Conocido::all()
ç=> [
     1 => "Juan",
   ]

>>> Conocido::find(1)
=> App\Models\Conocido {#4585
     +id: 1,
     +nombre: "Juan",
   }

>>> $encontrado = Conocido::find(1)
=> App\Models\Conocido {#4590
     +id: 1,
     +nombre: "Juan",
   }

>>> $encontrado->nombre = "Pedro"
=> "Pedro"

>>> $encontrado->save()
=> true

>>> Conocido::all()
=> [
     1 => "Pedro",
   ]

>>> exit
Exit:  Goodbye
```

Remember that Tinker is an interpreter so it does not need to conclude the lines with a ; and that it shows us the result of the statement we execute with enter.
Another concept that we will see will be a middleware, we will know its use and creation. First of all, let's see this as a filter that will inspect each of the requests that a client sends to the server, if certain conditions are met in the middleware then the request can continue with the request, but if not, some other action can be carried out.

This functionality can be used in several circumstances, for example when we want to be able to use the system in a certain region or at a certain time (within the data that a request has, we can check other factors such as the existence or not of some circumstance (in this case we will check the existence of a variable in the session), firstly to create it we will use the command

```
php artisan make:middleware ReviewSessionVariable
```

this creates the file RevisarVariableDeSession.php in the subfolder Middleware in the Http directory inside the app folder

and its contention is as follows:

```php
<?php

namespace App\Http\Middleware;

use Closure;
use Illuminate\Http\Request;

class RevisarVariableDeSession
{
    /**
     * Handle an incoming request.
     *
     * @param  \Illuminate\Http\Request  $request
     * @param  \Closure(\Illuminate\Http\Request): (\Illuminate\Http\Response|\Illuminate\Http\RedirectResponse)  $next
     * @return \Illuminate\Http\Response|\Illuminate\Http\RedirectResponse
     */
    public function handle(Request $request, Closure $next)
    {
        return $next($request);
    }
}
```

If we review it is a class but it has a method called handle that receives the request and by default returns a call to the next method passing it by parameter the request that we received, now in it we will implement the logic that if the data variable does not exist in the session we will return to the beginning.

```php
public function handle(Request $request, Closure $next)
{
    $data = session('data', null);
    if(is_null($data)) return redirect('/');
    return $next($request);
}
```

For this middleware to check all the requests that are made in our web system (when we navigate in it) we must register it (the reader should remember that in the Kernel.php file found in Http we commented the code so that it would not use the VerifyCsrfToken) so in the routeMiddleware array (a few lines later) we will add the reference to the class we have just created, and we will also assign it a name

```
    /**
     * The application's route middleware.
     *
     * These middleware may be assigned to groups or used individually.
     *
     * @var array<string, class-string|string>
     */
    protected $routeMiddleware = [
        'auth' => \App\Http\Middleware\Authenticate::class,
        'auth.basic' => \Illuminate\Auth\Middleware\AuthenticateWithBasicAuth::class,
        'auth.session' => \Illuminate\Session\Middleware\AuthenticateSession::class,
        'cache.headers' => \Illuminate\Http\Middleware\SetCacheHeaders::class,
        'can' => \Illuminate\Auth\Middleware\Authorize::class,
        'guest' => \App\Http\Middleware\RedirectIfAuthenticated::class,
        'password.confirm' => \Illuminate\Auth\Middleware\RequirePassword::class,
        'signed' => \App\Http\Middleware\ValidateSignature::class,
        'throttle' => \Illuminate\Routing\Middleware\ThrottleRequests::class,
        'verified' => \Illuminate\Auth\Middleware\EnsureEmailIsVerified::class,
        'revisar' => \App\Http\Middleware\RevisarVariableDeSession::class,
    ];
}
```

Now when we declare a path in our web.php file, we can filter access to it with the middleware check

```
Route::get('known',[ KnownController::class,'index'])->middleware('review');
```

Finally before going into more specific features of programming with LARAVEL we will know a concept that is the ORM (Object-relational mapping) is a technique in which all the elements of a database correspond to an object. In this way when we program (object-oriented) we can interact with the tables of our manager.

Laravel uses the ORM called ELOQUENT, as we saw before when we create a model with the **php artisan make:model** command we create a class that inherits from Model, so we are creating an entity and it will represent a table of our database and all the attributes of this class will represent the attributes of that table, as well as the key and foreign keys (at this moment ELOQUENT does not support the use of super keys).

In the previous exercise, we created methods such as save(), since the Model class also provides it.

3.- The configuration files

Laravel is a framework that privileges the conventions over the configuration, that is to say that if you give the elements the established names or include them in the position that was pre said things will work without needing to configure something, but not for this it is impossible to configure the behavior of the parts of the framework, in the last book we knew the file .env file (remember this is not installed with the framework, it must be created) and in it are the environment variables for our application to work how we want (within this file we will find several lines of the form VARIABLE=value (each variable in a different line as shown in Figure 1) are used in various configuration files (included in the config folder) in it we will find for example the database.php file (in which is written the configuration of how the framework interacts with the DBMS), for example in it is found

```
'default' => env('DB_CONNECTION', 'mysql'),
```

Just to explain the previous code, the operator => can be found in the syntax of assignment of the arrays in which we specify the value that will have an index, in the .env file you can establish that the type of connection to use is another (LARAVEL by default accepts that the connections are with the sqlite, mysql, pgsql or sqlsrv driver, these are the drivers that the framework has included but you can add others) then when the framework reads the configuration file database.php configuration file it will get an array in which the index named default has the value that is set in the .env (all configuration files return an array you can confirm this because they all start with return [ ).

A call to the env function not only we will see it in the database configuration file, also in others, for example in app.php, broadcasting.php, in cache.php, etc, what this function does is to receive two parameters, the first one is the name of an environment variable, the second one is optional and is the value that will return if the first one is not found in the configuration file .env, if it is not specified then it will return NULL.

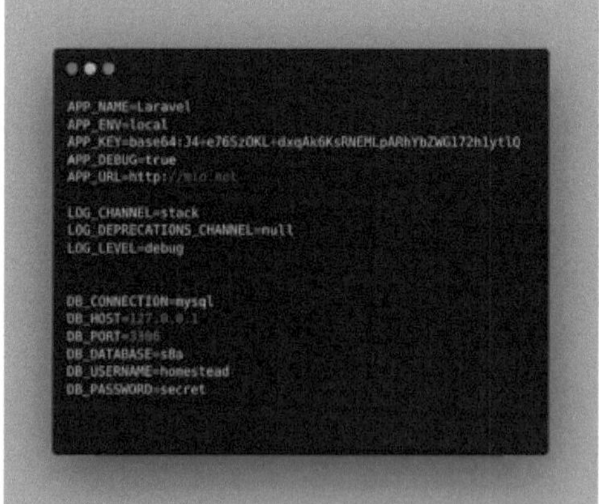

Figure 1 Example of .env file

4.- Using the database

As previously mentioned the framework incorporates support for SQLite, MySQL, pgsql or sqlsrv databases, by default it works with MySQL databases so it requires to specify the server, the port, the name of the database and the user as well as the password, in figure 1 we can see that the values were for a mysql connection were 127.0.0.1, 3306, s8a, homestead and secret, but we could easily change to use a different database management system for example a very simple one that uses a file (SQLite) and the only thing we would have to write is:

```
DB_CONNECTION=sqlite
```

and we would no longer use the other variables (host, port, databasename, username, password)

This will cause the framework to look for a file called database.sqlite inside the database folder (as shown in figure 2).

Figure 2 File for the database

If we want to use a special file to save our database we can do it with the variable DB_DATABASE, remember that the name of the file is specified and it will be in the root of the project.

It is not necessary to assign a host in case of SQLite since it is a database management system that is minimal and works within the host itself, it does not do so in the client-server architecture.

5.- Creation of models

In a previous post we already mentioned the models, it is time to see them more in depth, using the artisan script we can create one using the php artisan make:model Docente command, this creates the file Docente.php (with a class called Docente), remember that by convention (not by rule since if we don't follow it anyway the file will be created, but we will have to configure more things) the name must be in singular and written in pascalcase . [15]

```
<?php

namespace AppModels;

use Illuminate "Database" to create an Illuminate "Factories" factory;
use Illuminate "Database";

class Teacher extends Model
{
    use HasFactory;
}
```

A class called Teacher is created that inherits from the Model class (the latter is an implementation of the ORM[16] elocuent), so the newly created class has access to methods (static or instance) that allow it to interact with the database management system that has been defined (MySQL by default) and we will not have to worry about aspects such as connecting to the database server, knowing the instructions to retrieve data from it or how to delete them; If to an instance we say ->save() its content will be saved in the persistent storage, in some occasions a client can request to make a program to use its data, it can provide us the databases, and it will be necessary to adapt us to its tables.

When we create an eloquent model it expects that the table with which it interacts will be named snakecase[17] and it is the plural of the model name, in this case it would look for a table called teachers but let's suppose that the school asks us to use their teachers catalog, so we must adapt our code to the table they provide us.

[15] This is a naming convention that indicates that identifiers should be written in lower case except for the first letter of each word which should be in upper case, for example if we define a variable to count the number of blue cars we could call this BlueCarts

[16] This is a way of programming in which all database elements are mapped to object-oriented programming.

[17] This is a naming convention that indicates that identifiers should be written in lower case and all occurrences of spaces should be replaced by underscores, for example if we define a variable to count the number of blue cars we could call this blue_carts

```
mysql> desc profesor;
+--------------+-------------+------+-----+---------+-------+
| Field        | Type        | Null | Key | Default | Extra |
+--------------+-------------+------+-----+---------+-------+
| RFCsimple    | varchar(10) | NO   | PRI | NULL    |       |
| Nombre       | varchar(45) | YES  |     | NULL    |       |
| Apat         | varchar(45) | YES  |     | NULL    |       |
| Amat         | varchar(45) | YES  |     | NULL    |       |
| FechaIngreso | varchar(45) | YES  |     | NULL    |       |
+--------------+-------------+------+-----+---------+-------+
5 rows in set (0.00 sec)
```

Figure 3 Teacher" table provided by the school

The next thing we will specify is that the primary key is not called "id" as eloquent would expect is the RFCsimple column (another thing that is expected is that the key attribute is of type integer and is auto incremental), another aspect is that eloquent looks for 2 fields one called created_at and another updated_at that automatically store the date and time that the record was created and updated respectively and in our case if we have a field that meets this and is "FechaIngreso", the model will also configure this field.

```
<?php

namespace AppModels;

use Illuminate "Database";

class Teacher extends Model
{
    protected $table="teacher";
    protected $primaryKey = 'RFCsimple';
    public $incrementing = false;
    protected $keyType = 'string';
// public $timestamps = false;
    const CREATED_AT = 'FechaIngreso';
    const UPDATED_AT = null;
}
```

With all this we have configured the previous model specifying the name of the table that will be used, as it has a key attribute that is not called id we also specify it, and since this is not an auto incremental integer we specify this and that it is of type string, as we do not want to disable the record that eloquent makes we do not tell it not to use this feature (with the commented line) instead we are specifying which is the field that will take the place of created_at

Now we will use the tinker tool (a command line that allows to interpret and execute PHP code) to execute LARAVEL code (it interprets PHP code and as the framework is based on this language it also interprets it), which we will explain:

Inside the project folder we must execute the `php artisan tinker` command

```
Psy Shell v0.11.12 (PHP 8.2.1 — cli) by Justin Hileman
> App\Models\Docente::find('GUSJ');
= App\Models\Docente {#4683
    RFCsimple: "GUSJ",
    Nombre: "Jose",
    Apat: "Gutiérrez",
    Amat: "Suarez",
    FechaIngreso: "2020-04-15",
  }
```

Figure 4 Retrieving a record from the table

With this model we can interact with the database.

```
> $nuevo = new App\Models\Docente();
= App\Models\Docente {#4679}

> $nuevo->RFCsimple="RAPK";
= "RAPK"

> $nuevo->nombre = "Karla";
= "Karla"

> $nuevo->Apat = "Rámirez"
= "Rámirez"

> $nuevo->Amat = "Pérez"
= "Pérez"

> $nuevo->save();
= true
```

Figure 5 Adding a new record

And in the database we have

```
mysql> select * from profesor;
+-----------+--------+-----------+--------+--------------+
| RFCsimple | Nombre | Apat      | Amat   | FechaIngreso |
+-----------+--------+-----------+--------+--------------+
| GUSJ      | Jose   | Gutiérrez | Suarez | 2020-04-15   |
| RAPK      | Karla  | Rámirez   | Pérez  | 2023-04-04   |
+-----------+--------+-----------+--------+--------------+
2 rows in set (0.00 sec)
```

But if we have the opportunity to create the database we will use all the tools that LARAVEL gives us to model it.

If we use the php artisan help make:model command we will get a message like the one shown below:

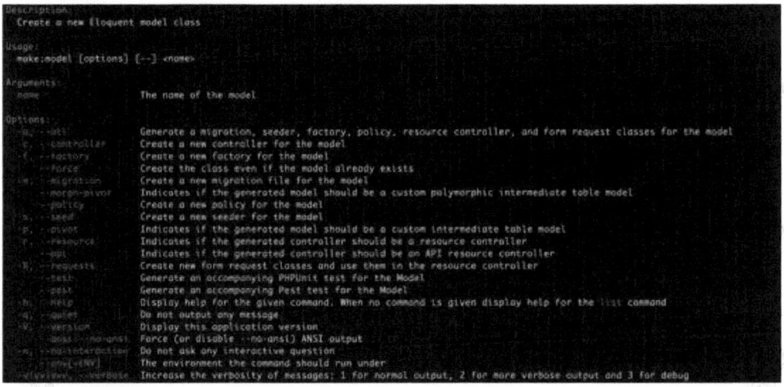

```
Description:
  Create a new Eloquent model class

Usage:
  make:model [options] [--] <name>

Arguments:
  name                  The name of the model

Options:
  -a, --all             Generate a migration, seeder, factory, policy, resource controller, and form request classes for the model
  -c, --controller      Create a new controller for the model
  -f, --factory         Create a new factory for the model
      --force           Create the class even if the model already exists
  -m, --migration       Create a new migration file for the model
      --morph-pivot     Indicates if the generated model should be a custom polymorphic intermediate table model
      --policy          Create a new policy for the model
  -s, --seed            Create a new seeder for the model
  -p, --pivot           Indicates if the generated model should be a custom intermediate table model
  -r, --resource        Indicates if the generated controller should be a resource controller
      --api             Indicates if the generated controller should be an API resource controller
  -R, --requests        Create new form request classes and use them in the resource controller
      --test            Generate an accompanying PHPUnit test for the Model
      --pest            Generate an accompanying Pest test for the Model
  -h, --help            Display help for the given command. When no command is given display help for the list command
  -q, --quiet           Do not output any message
  -V, --version         Display this application version
      --ansi|--no-ansi  Force (or disable --no-ansi) ANSI output
  -n, --no-interaction  Do not ask any interactive question
      --env[=ENV]       The environment the command should run under
  -v|vv|vvv, --verbose  Increase the verbosity of messages: 1 for normal output, 2 for more verbose output and 3 for debug
```

Creating the control for a model

In the help we can see the options that we can use with the command, although the most comfortable is to use the option --all (I use the options in its long form because in the short form not all have their equivalent) we will use the command php artisan make:model --controller Docente we will get a message telling us that not only the file Docente.php was created in the models folder, but also the file DocenteController.php (remember that the name of a controller can come from a use case or from a model) in the controllers folder (this controller is empty and in it we must implement the methods used to interact (the convention states that all the methods must be in camelcase[18]), but if what we will perform will be the operations of the CRUD[19] then instead we can use the --resource option that will create the code of the controller already with the methods index, create, store, show, edit, update, destroy, these methods require implementation, but the "shell" is created. This controller makes use of a characteristic that the framework knows as "Route Model Binding" that is to say, for example, the method show whose definition is:

```
public function show(Teacher $teacher)
{
}
```

It will be called when the user uses the following path (the declarations and parameter passing even though we already covered it in a previous edition we will explain it again and expand on it)

```
Route::get('teachers/{teacher?}/show',[TeacherController::class, 'show']);
```

The route declared above is defining that it reacts to get type requests, it will execute the show method of the DocenteController class when the request complies with the URI indicating the key number of the teacher. Thanks to the "Route Model Binding" what the framework does is that the parameter (teacher number) will be the id of the model and

[18] This is a naming convention that indicates that identifiers must be written in lower case except for the first letter of each word that is not the first, for example if you define a method that is to measure the temperature you could call this measureTemperature

[19] They are the actions that are performed on a persistent storage (commonly we will say on the database), this is an acronym for Create, Read, Update and Delete.

then it executes Teacher::find(teacher), if the id does not exist in the table it returns an error of type 404 since it is used to a FindOrFail,

To clarify the example we could define the following path:

```
Route::get('present/{which?}',[DocenteController::class, 'show']);
```

In this path we define that the parameter is the variable which and that the method show will be executed, in its implementation we will have to execute the line that looks for the record.

```
public function show($which){
    $teacher = Teacher::findOrFail($which);
    //implementation code
}
```

For the "Route Model Binding" to work we must call the parameter as the entity and in lower case.

Creating a migration for a model

The next option that we will address is -migration, migrations are a simile to the DDL of SQL[20] because in these we can describe the tables, the convention states that the tables and fields of the databases will be named using snakecase, if we use the php command artisan make:model -migration Docente in addition to creating the model will originate a file within the sub folder migrations of the database folder, this will be in a file whose name will be of the form <date><action>.php, the file name indicates the time when the migration is being created and the action it performs, in this example we have a file called 2023_04_02_011600_create_docentes_table.php, this time we see that does not respect that the file name is the name of the class since it generates an anonymous class that contains two methods, **up** for the time when migrations are executed and **down** to undo the changes they make.

Generally these will be used to create tables, that is why the name, the Scheme class that represents the schema of the database is used, we have the call to the create function whose action is the same as a SQL CREATE TABLE, instead it indicates both the name of the table to create and the fields it will contain, by default when a migration is created there are two functions, one is id that indicates that a field called id is created, it is an unsigned and incremental integer (by convention the name of the key attribute of a table eloquent will look for it as id and in the case of foreign keys the name will be formed with the name of the entity to which they refer followed by the word id (take into account several aspects, first of all that we use the name of the entity to which they refer followed by the word id), firstly that we use the name of the entity not the table, another is that by convention all attribute names are in snake case) and we also have the call to the timestamps function that what it does is to indicate that you must create the fields created_at and updated_at both of timpo timestapm and that by default will save the time when a record is created or updated.

```
public function up()
{
    Schema::create('teachers', function (Blueprint $table) {
        $table->id();
        $table->string("name");
        $table->string("father_surname");
        $table->date("contract_date");
    });
```

[20] The structured query language has 5 types of commands (DDL, DML, DCL, TCL, DQL), the first one (Data Definition Language) groups those that allow to define the structure of the tables, the characteristics of the tables and fields (CREATE, ALTER, DROP, TRUNCATE, RENAME).

```
}
```

We can make modifications in tables already created, for example in the teachers table we will create a migration to add a field for the paternal surname, then we will use the command php artisan make:migration add_field_for_paternal_surname_to_teacher --table=teachers, in the same way a file is created and contains two methods, in the **up** we will put:

```
public function up()
{
    Schema::table('teachers', function (Blueprint $table) {
        $table->string("mother_name")->after('father_name');
    });
}
```

The afeter method assigns that the new field must be after the father_surname field, otherwise it will be created after hire_date.

Aggregating data for a model

Another option is --seed (we will not use the --factory) even though both allow to create records in the database the difference between seeders and factories is that the latter add records with random values while in the former the values are predefined by the programmer. If we use the command php artisan make:model -seed Docente we will also create the file DocenteSeeder.php in the sub folder seeders of the datbase folder, inside the created class we will find a method run, which will be the one that will be executed when we run the seeders, here we will write the code with which we add new teachers.

```
public function run()
{
    $docente = new Docente();
    teacher->name = "John";
    teacher->paternal_surname = "Lopez";
    teacher->maternal_surname = "Rodriguez";
    $teacher->save();
    $docente = new Docente();
    teacher->name = "Ana";
    teacher->paternal_surname = "Perez";
    teacher->maternal_surname = "Ruíz";
    $teacher->save();
    $docente = new Docente();
    teacher->name = "Ricardo";
    teacher->paternal_surname = "Lopez";
    $docente->apellido_materno = "Hernández";
    $teacher->save();
    $docente = new Docente();
    teacher->name = "Laura";
    teacher->paternal_surname = "Perez";
    $docente->apellido_materno = "Sarmiento";
    $teacher->save();
}
```

But in the DatabaseSeeder class within the run method we must call the class DocenteSeeder, we do this with the following code:

```
public function run()
{
    $this->call(TeacherSeeder::class);
    // \AppmodelsUser::factory(10)->create();

    // \AppApps "Models" "User::factory()->create([
    // 'name' => 'Test User',
    // 'email' => 'test@example.com',
    // ]);
}
```

For the moment we will see only these options of the make:model command, we will create the database with the tables teachers and subjects, now we will see the relationships that can be had between models.

Relationships between models

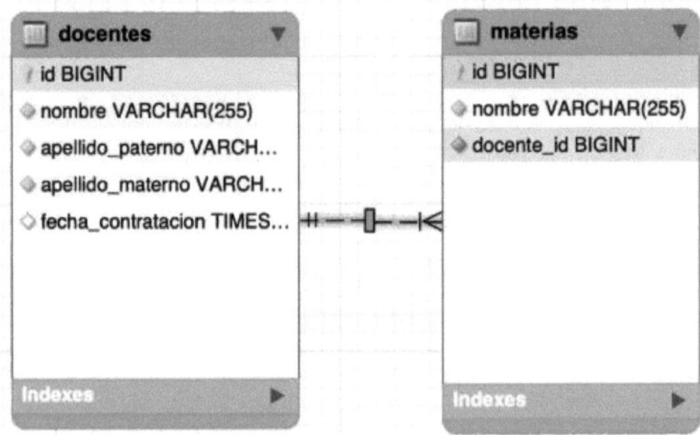

We have already discussed how to create the migrations and configure the model of the Teacher, now we will create the entity Subject, how the convention calls for the key field for each table is called id, is auto incremental and an integer (large integer) unsigned, the table of subjects will have a field that will be foreign key so its name is docente_id since it refers to the id field of the teaching entity and is named in snakecase), the fields, the migration for this entity will be:

```
Schema::create('subjects', function (Blueprint $table) {
    $table->id();
    $table->string("name");
    $table->unsignedBigInteger("docente_id");
    $table->foreign("docente_id", "fk_docente")
          ->on("teachers")
          ->references("id");
});
```

In the creation we are adding a large unsigned integer (since it must be of the same type as the field to which they refer and the key fields generated by the id() function are of this type, another method that we could judge as new is the foreign one that allows to establish a foreign key to which we must indicate to which table it will refer and the field with which it will be matched.

The name fk_teacher is the name that will be assigned to the index that is created for a foreign key. remember that you can create indexes for one or more fields.

We have created the seeder and configured the model to not use the timestapms, the records that we have in the table are the following:

```
mysql> select * from materias;
+----+-------------------------------+------------+
| id | nombre                        | docente_id |
+----+-------------------------------+------------+
|  1 | Redes                         |          1 |
|  2 | Programacion                  |          2 |
|  3 | Fundamentos de Base de datos  |          3 |
+----+-------------------------------+------------+
3 rows in set (0.00 sec)
```

It is now time to configure the relationships in the models, we will do this by creating methods (which by convention will be named as what we expect to obtain) and in them we will return the related objects.

One-to-one relationships

Now it is time to configure the relationships between models, the simplest and first we will see is the one to one, which in this case is said that the teaching model has a subject, the relationship is hasOne, if we follow the conventions the configuration of the relationships will be almost null, without being necessary to specify table names or models or keys, or other extra data.

In the Teacher's model we will create the method

```
public function materia(){
    return $this->hasOne("AppModelsMatter");
}
```

If in our models involved we had not respected the conventions it would be necessary to specify the foreign and local keys, remember that the subject method is created in the Teacher model) is teacher_id and that it refers to the id field of the Subject model.

```
public function materia(){
    return $this->hasOne("AppModelsSubject",'teacher_id','id');
}
```

```
Psy Shell v0.11.12 (PHP 8.2.1 — cli) by Justin Hileman
> Docente::find(1)->materia
[!] Aliasing 'Docente' to 'App\Models\Docente' for this Tinker session.
= App\Models\Materia {#4687
    id: 1,
    nombre: "Redes",
    docente_id: 1,
  }
```

Figure 6 Checking the material method

In depth hasOne realtion

```
Psy Shell v0.11.12 (PHP 8.2.1 — cli) by Justin Hileman
> Docente::find(1)->materia
[!] Aliasing 'Docente' to 'App\Models\Docente' for this Tinker session.
= App\Models\Materia {#4687
    id: 1,
    nombre: "Redes",
    docente_id: 1,
  }

> Docente::find(1)->materia()
= Illuminate\Database\Eloquent\Relations\HasOne {#4690}

> Docente::find(1)->materia()->first()
= App\Models\Materia {#4695
    id: 1,
    nombre: "Redes",
    docente_id: 1,
  }
```

Figure 7 In reality there is the method matter, not the attribute (the property).

Explaining in detail, all these methods return an object of type relation, but php has some methods known as magic methods, when we try to access to the property matter that in fact does not exist, what we declare is the function matter, this one is executed and returns an object of type relation, which when executing it we can obtain the result.

If we do the above on the teacher 4 (which is not associated to any subject) the result will be null, but a feature of the hasOne class is that we can set a default value for the result when it is null, then we must modify the method code:

```
public function materia(){
    return $this->hasOne("AppModelsMatter")
    ->withDefault(
        [
            "name" => "No matter",
            "id" => 0,
        ]
    );
}
```

To test this new modification we will use the tinker tool (this is an interpreter that needs to be reloaded to take modifications, if you are testing and you are using the tool you must exit it with the exit command and load it again).

```
Psy Shell v0.11.12 (PHP 8.2.1 — cli) by Justin Hileman
> Docente::find(4)->materia
[!] Aliasing 'Docente' to 'App\Models\Docente' for this Tinker session.
= App\Models\Materia {#4669
    docente_id: 4,
    nombre: "Sin materia",
    id: 0,
  }
```

Figure 8 Checking withDefault

Inverse of the relationship

The inverse of the hasOne relationship is belongsTo so we will modify the Subject model to include a teaching method (if before it was shown that a teacher has a subject, now the inverse tells us that a subject belongs to a teacher):

```
public function teacher(){
   return $this->belongsTo('AppModelsTeacher');
}
```

If the conventions are not respected, we must specify the names of the key attributes, but also the convention indicates that the name of the method must be the name of the entity expected to be obtained.

```
public function master(){
   return $this->belongsTo('AppModelsTeacher','teacher_id', 'id') ;
}
```

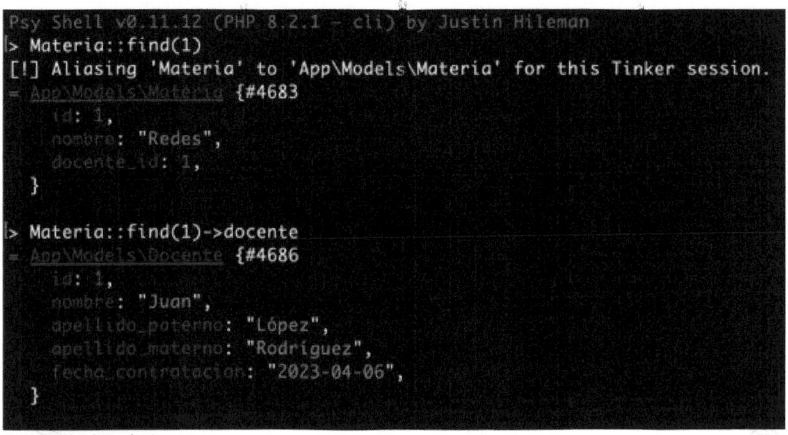

```
Psy Shell v0.11.12 (PHP 8.2.1 — cli) by Justin Hileman
> Materia::find(1)
[!] Aliasing 'Materia' to 'App\Models\Materia' for this Tinker session.
= App\Models\Materia {#4683
    id: 1,
    nombre: "Redes",
    docente_id: 1,
  }

> Materia::find(1)->docente
= App\Models\Docente {#4686
    id: 1,
    nombre: "Juan",
    apellido_paterno: "López",
    apellido_materno: "Rodríguez",
    fecha_contratacion: "2023-04-06",
  }
```

Figure 9 Checking the inverse

In-depth belongsTo relationship

Recall that calling the method returns an object of type relation which is executed, but there is also the toSql method that allows us to know the query to be executed.

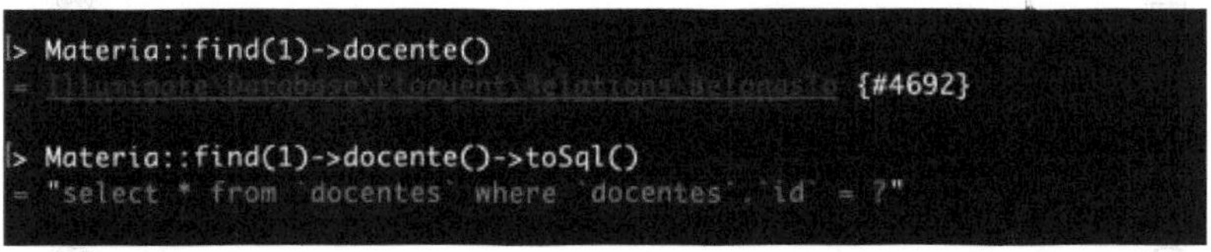

```
> Materia::find(1)->docente()
= Illuminate\Database\Eloquent\Relations\BelongsTo {#4692}

> Materia::find(1)->docente()->toSql()
= "select * from `docentes` where `docentes`.`id` = ?"
```

That question mark has to do with "bindig parameters" in php SQL queries, if you want to investigate that.

One-to-many relationships

We can easily implement a one-to-many relationship, we will use the same structure, but we will have different data:

```
mysql> select * from materias;
+----+-----------------------------------+------------+
| id | nombre                            | docente_id |
+----+-----------------------------------+------------+
|  1 | Redes                             |          1 |
|  2 | Conmutación                       |          1 |
|  3 | Programación                      |          2 |
|  4 | Programación Web                  |          2 |
|  5 | Fundamentos de Bases de datos     |          3 |
|  6 | Taller Bases de datos             |          3 |
|  7 | Administracion de Bases de datos  |          3 |
|  8 | Optativa                          |       NULL |
+----+-----------------------------------+------------+
8 rows in set (0.00 sec)
```

Now the Teacher model will have a subject method that should return the list of subjects in which a teacher is referenced, if the teacher has no assigned subjects the response will be an empty collection (the methods must have a name that semantically indicates what we expect to obtain).

```
public function subjects(){
    return $this->hasMany("AppModelsMatter");
}
```

```
Psy Shell v0.11.12 (PHP 8.2.1 — cli) by Justin Hileman
> Docente::find(2)->materias
[!] Aliasing 'Docente' to 'App\Models\Docente' for this Tinker session.
= Illuminate\Database\Eloquent\Collection {#4686
    all: [
      App\Models\Materia {#4689
        id: 3,
        nombre: "Programacion",
        docente_id: 2,
      },
      App\Models\Materia {#4690
        id: 4,
        nombre: "Programación Web",
        docente_id: 2,
      },
    ],
  }
```


We can continue using the belongsTo relation (that we use in the teaching method) which is the inverse also, since if it was expressed that a teacher has several subjects we will understand that in the inverse a subject belongs to a teacher.

Many-to-many relationships

When we have a many-to-many relationship this is broken into two one-to-many relationships, the solution is to create an intermediate table, this table is known as a pivot table with which we can know the subjects in which a student is enrolled and vice versa the students who are enrolled in a certain subject. and remembering that by convention the database tables are named in snakecase, another convention in this case would be that the pivot tables carry the name of the entities involved in ascending alphabetical order.

We will add one more entity to our example this will be the Student entity and in the enrollment there is a many to many relationship (many students enroll in many subjects), for this we create the entity Student and create several records.

Figure 10 Schematic of a many-to-many relationship

Optionally we will create the Inscripcion model but we will use the --pivot option, with this we will create a model but this one does not inherit from the Model class but uses the Pivot class (this second one inherits from the first one but implements several more methods).

Being pivot does not follow the convention that the name of the table is the name of the model in plural and in lowercase but it allows to overwrite it using the protected variable with the name of the table so we will create the table student_materia so we will also create the migration (it will be necessary to make some changes since if we use the php command `artisan make:model -pivot --migration Inscripcion` the table that is created in the migration is called inscripcion:

```
Schema::create('student_subject', function (Blueprint $table) {
    $table->id();
    $table->unsignedBigInteger("student_id");
    $table->unsignedBigInteger("materia_id");
    $table->float("average")->nullable()->default(null);
    $table->foreign("student_id", "fk_student")
    ->on("students")
    ->references("id");
    $table->foreign("materia_id", "fk_materia")
    ->on("subjects")
    ->references("id");
    $table->timestamps();
});
```

Pivots do not always have data other than foreign keys.

Hugo and Luis will be enrolled in Networking, Paco and Juan will be enrolled in Database Fundamentals and all students will be taking Programming (but the last one will be assigned an average of 80, this is for future use).

If we review the model we will see that the many-to-many relationship was broken into two one-to-many relationships and we can modify the models, In the Student model we create the method subjects:

```
public function subjects(){
    return $this->belongsToMany(Materia::class);
}
```

and in the Materia model we created the Materia method:

```
public function students(){
    return $this->belongsToMany(Student::class);
}
```

If we observe it is not necessary to write the name of the table since by convention the one that is looked for exists is called student_subject but if we have not respected it how second parameter we should indicate it, a method that exists is withPivot which allows to specify if we want some field in special in the pivot, since without it what is returned is a list of objects and inside each one of them an attribute is called pivot which contains the foreign keys, reason why the for a future use the first relation would be like this:

```
public function subjects(){
    return $this->belongsToMany(Subject::class)->withPivot('average');
}
```

Type relationships through

We have methods hasOneThrough and hasManyThrough, both allow to get the related record(s) through a table (but receive an intermediate model).

For this example a new entity has been introduced, the thematic contents, this entity has a relationship with subjects (in this case it is one to one) but since the teaching entity is related to the subject, it is transitive that the teacher is related to the content, therefore we can know what contents a specific teacher should cover.

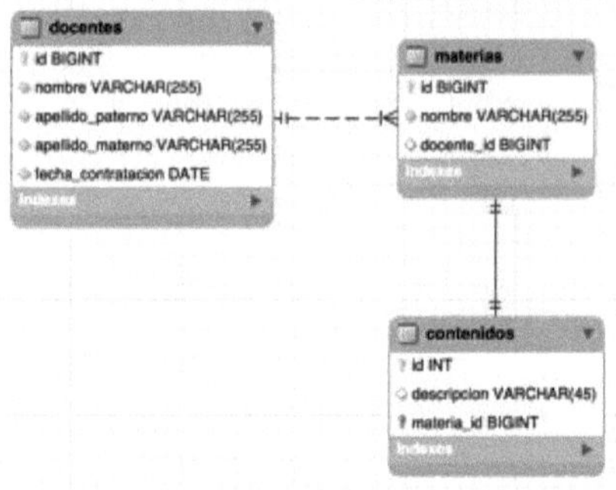

To implement this we must create a method called contents (we commented that it is by convention not by rule that we must name in a certain way the methods that implement relationships) that returns a hasOneThrough object that depending on the context could be a hasManyThrough since its configuration is similar.

```
public function contents(){
    return $this->hasOneThrough(
        Content::class,
        Subject::class
    );
}
```

We will use again the php artisan tinker command to check the operation established before:

```
Psy Shell v0.11.12 (PHP 8.2.1 — cli) by Justin Hileman
> Docente::find(1)->contenidos
[!] Aliasing 'Docente' to 'App\Models\Docente' for this Tinker session.
= App\Models\Contenido {#4686
    id: 1,
    descripcion: """
      1.- Introducción a redes de datos. \n
              2.- Normas y estándares de redes de datos.\n
              3.- Dispositivos de red.
      """,
    materia_id: 1,
    created_at: "2023-04-10 01:03:01",
    updated_at: "2023-04-10 01:03:01",
    laravel_through_key: 1,
  }
```

Figure 11 Checking the hasOneThrough method

There are also polymorphic relationships, which we will not discuss in this paper.

Emulate certain types of relationships by modifying parameters

We could find ourselves with an inherited database design (i.e. we did not make it) and therefore we must mainly configure our models, by configuring our relation methods it is possible to obtain certain results even when we use other functions, what this refers to is that we can obtain the result of a type of relation using a function of another type by simply adding the appropriate parameters.

For example:

```
public function materia(){
    return $this->hasOne("AppModelsMatter");
}
```

Configuring:

```
public function materia(){
    return $this->belongsTo("AppModelsMatter", "id", "matter_id");
}
```

Or we can consider that a number of students have a certain subject through enrollment (actually this was the case for the many-to-many relationship) but we could solve this in the Subject model as follows:

```
public function students(){
    return $this->hasManyThrough(
        Student::class,
        Registration::class,
        'matter_id',
        'id',
        'id',
        'student_id',
    );
}
```

6.- Querying the database

Using models and the querybuilder

In some occasions it is necessary to make queries directly to the database, actually the relations are certain queries, as well as certain methods are also queries, for example when we do Model::all() what we are doing is a "SELECT * FROM models", there is a method that every model has called query(), this returns an object of type Builder, this has a method called toSql() that returns the query in SQL that has been constructed, to the query you can add clauses where and other modifications to obtain the sentence that is required. Remember that by executing the toSql() function we can obtain the result.

Let's check the above:

```
Psy Shell v0.11.12 (PHP 8.2.1 — cli) by Justin Hileman
> $consulta = Docente::query();
[!] Aliasing 'Docente' to 'App\Models\Docente' for this Tinker session.
= Illuminate\Database\Eloquent\Builder {#4677}

> $consulta->where('apellido_paterno','López');
= Illuminate\Database\Eloquent\Builder {#4677}

> $consulta->toSql();
= "select * from `docentes` where `apellido_paterno` = ?"

> $consulta->get();
= Illuminate\Database\Eloquent\Collection {#4681
    all: [
      App\Models\Docente {#4667
        id: 1,
        nombre: "Juan",
        apellido_paterno: "López",
        apellido_materno: "Rodriguez",
        fecha_contratacion: "2023-04-10",
      },
      App\Models\Docente {#4685
        id: 3,
        nombre: "Ricardo",
        apellido_paterno: "López",
        apellido_materno: "Hernández",
        fecha_contratacion: "2023-04-10",
      },
    ],
  }
```

Figure 12 Query with where

Using the database

LARAVEL provides an abstraction of the database and with it we can make use of the DBMS directly, for this we must build our own queries, the topic that we will see is the QueryBuilder (Illuminate Database QueryBuilder) This class also has methods toSql and get and allows us to make more elaborate queries (those in which we want to filter, group and other things that we want directly with SQL), another characteristic is that we can carry out transactions on the database, remember that a transaction in database is a set of queries that are executed as if they were only one to respect the ACID principles (Acronym of the English that takes the initials of each one of the characteristics of a transaction: Atomicity, remember that a transaction is several queries, they are executed all or none, that is to say if one fails, they all fail, Consistency means that after being executed the database will continue sinedo consistent, Isolate means that a transaction is executed in isolation from the others and its modifications are not visible until it has been confirmed and Durability means that a transaction lasts once it has been positively resolved), this is not a DATABASE course, so we will not go deeper into the concepts of this subject or the SQL language so we will explain how a query can be used with the QUERY BUILDER.

We can make use of it thanks to the DB class (use Illuminate\Support\Facades\DB;), to execute a query, e.g.

The following query

```
SELECT subjects.name, students.name FROM students INNER JOIN student_subject ON students.id =
student_subject.student_id INNER JOIN subjects ON student_subject.subject_id = subject.id
```

We could use it like this

```
//previous code
$query = DB::table('students')
        ->join('student_subject','students.id','=','student_subject.student_id')
        ->join('subjects', 'student_subject.subject_id', '=', 'subjects.id')
        ->select('subjects.name','students.name');
//next code
```

The advantage of the DB abstraction is that the result is independent of the database manager we use, for example if we use Sql Server the language would be TransactSQL and if we use other systems such as PostgreSQL, there are differences even if they are minimal in each implementation, for example to limit the number of rows returned in a query in Mysql we use the LIMIT clause but in Sql Server the TOP clause is used.

Personally, after 5 years of using the framework, there are less and less occasions in which I think it is necessary to use the QueryBuilder, such as transactions.

Transactions

For example to delete a student just execute $student->delete() but this should not be done unless the student is not enrolled in any subject, for this we would use the transactions, first we would initiate a transaction, then we delete the enrollments that this one could have, and we finish the transaction, but if there is some error (or some reason for which the operations could not be carried out) then the changes are canceled. For example, an enrollment could not be deleted if it has a grade (we will use a method called enrollments that returns a relation of type hasMany since a student has several enrollments).

A first attempt at the Student model controller would be:

```
public function destroy(Student $student)
{
    foreach( $student->enrollment as $enrollment ){
        if (is_null($inscription->average)) $inscription->delete();
    }
    $student->delete();
    return redirect(route('students.index'));
}
```

And we could confirm that it works for the student Luis, but with Juan it will fail (remember that to Juan we have assigned him an average of 80 in the enrollment to Programming), it is here where we could use one more feature of the PHP language, which is the handling of exceptions together with the transactions since with the code as it is shown the result will be that the student Juan is only enrolled in the subject Programming. The deletion method now looks like this:

```
public function destroy(Student $student)
{
   DB::beginTransaction();
   try {
      foreach( $student->enrollment as $enrollment ){
         if (is_null($inscription->average)) $inscription->delete();
      }
      $student->delete();
      DB::commit();
   } catch (\Throwable $th) {
      DB::rollBack();
   }
   return redirect(route('students.index'));
}
```

Sub-queries

In rare occasions it will be necessary to make a complex query (how it was seen can be made use of the database, but personally I recommend to make use of the models since these provide a greater abstraction of the database and a better semantics is obtained, but it will be necessary to use for example the sub queries, we will make use of a code that demonstrates it:

```
static public function assets(){
   return Teacher::whereIn('id',function ($query)
            {
               $query->select('docente_id')
               ->from('teacher_subject');
            })->get();
}
```

In the previous block a static function was defined within the Teacher model that returns only those teachers who have been assigned a subject, we are making a sub-query since the result is the execution of the query:

```
SELECT * FROM `teachers` WHERE `id` IN (SELECT `teacher_id` FROM `teacher_subject`)
```

7.- Other programming practices

In order to achieve a successful application we will make use of multiple technologies, languages, etc. For example, if you make a site it will have a better appearance thanks to the css styles that you can apply, in the same way it will increase the interactivity thanks to java script, and it will be able to communicate with other services through Apis Rest.

Create an API (Application Program Inteface).

LARAVEL being a full stack framework allows to implement apis, similar to how the routes were created for the web application (in the web.php file) we have an api.php file, the difference is that these routes only receive and return data, we never implement one to show certain interface (the views) and in the same way that we have resource type controllers we will have api type controllers that have by default the methods for the CRUD (index, store, update, show, update and destroy). We will create the controller for the Api, it is not a rule or convention, but in this example we will call it with the prefix Api, similar to the resource type controllers using the `php` command `artisan make:controller -model=Docente --api ApiDocenteController` we get the "shell" of a controller to manage the model, remember that we only receive data (usually through the request) and return data (in json format), the path will be created in the api.php file.

```
Route::apiResource('teachers', ApiDocenteController::class);
```

Now we will implement the api, remember that instead of returning the data to the view we return it in json format, to show this let's compare our Docent controllers

```
public function index()
{
    $todos = Docente::all();
    return view("teachers.index",compact('all'));
}
```

Against our api controller

```
public function index()
{
    return Teacher::all()->toJson();
}
```

In order to make use of this data we can implement an application in any language that supports api calls, it can be a mobile app, a java desktop program or a web application in any other framework, even a frot end framework such as Vue.js (later we will give an example with this one).

The following code is the records in json format (this stands for Java Script Objetc Notation and is the standard for sharing data between web services, since it is in plain text and easy to understand).


```
[
  {
    "id": 1,
    "name": "Jose",
    "height": 1.8,
    "created_at": "2023-04-17T06:18:15.000000Z",
    "updated_at": "2023-04-17T06:18:15.000000Z",
    "username": "jdocente",
    "key":"$2y$10$92IXUNpkjO0rOQ5byMi.Ye4oKoEa3Ro9llC/.og/at2.uheWG/igi",
    "image": "jose.jpg"
  },
  {
    "id": 2,
    "name": "Ana",
    "height": 1.6,
    "created_at": "2023-04-17T06:18:15.000000Z",
```

```
        "updated_at": "2023-04-17T06:18:15.000000Z",
        "username": "adocente",
        "key":"$2y$10$92IXUNpkjO0rOQ5byMi.Ye4oKoEa3Ro9llC/.og/at2.uheWG/igi",
        "image": "ana.jpg"
    },
    {
        "id": 3,
        "name": "Ricardo",
        "height": 1.7,
        "created_at": "2023-04-17T06:18:15.000000Z",
        "updated_at": "2023-04-17T06:18:15.000000Z",
        "username": "rdocente",
        "key":"$2y$10$92IXUNpkjO0rOQ5byMi.Ye4oKoEa3Ro9llC/.og/at2.uheWG/igi",
        "image": "ricardo.jpg"
    },
    {
        "id": 4,
        "name": "Laura",
        "height": 1.7,
        "created_at": "2023-04-17T06:18:15.000000Z",
        "updated_at": "2023-04-17T06:18:15.000000Z",
        "username": "ldocente",
        "key":"$2y$10$92IXUNpkjO0rOQ5byMi.Ye4oKoEa3Ro9llC/.og/at2.uheWG/igi",
        "image": "laura.jpg"
    }
]
```

Remembering the relationships we can see that each one of them is interconnected with the subjects it teaches and we have a method called subjects and we want that information to be sent in the json so we will modify our index

```
public function index()
{
    return Teacher::with('subjects')->get()->toJson();
}
```

The changes that we can observe firstly is that we call the method with indicating the relation that we want to load, how this returns us an object of type Builder will be necessary to execute it for that reason the call to the function get finally how before we return this in format json.

```
[
    {
        "id": 1,
        "name": "Jose",
        "height": 1.8,
        "created_at": "2023-04-17T06:18:15.000000Z",
        "updated_at": "2023-04-17T06:18:15.000000Z",
        "username": "jdocente",
        "key":"$2y$10$92IXUNpkjO0rOQ5byMi.Ye4oKoEa3Ro9llC/.og/at2.uheWG/igi",
        "image": "jose.jpg",
        "materials": [
            {
                "id": 1,
                "name": "Networks",
                "docente_id": 1,
                "created_at": "2023-04-17T06:18:15.000000Z",
                "updated_at": "2023-04-17T06:18:15.000000Z"
            },
            {
                "id": 2,
                "name: "Commutation",
                "docente_id": 1,
                "created_at": "2023-04-17T06:18:15.000000Z",
                "updated_at": "2023-04-17T06:18:15.000000Z"
            }
```

```
    ]
  },
...
]
```

Data validation.

For this feature it is necessary to use the Accept: application/json header to indicate to the server that will process the request that what is returned is a json otherwise what will happen is that if the validation fails it will return to the previous page and the session will have all the errors found.

The feature we are talking about are the "FormRequests" which are validators and with the `php artisan make:request StoreDocenteRequest` (convention dictates that the file name should be <action><Model>Request) the StoreDocenteRequest file is created in the Requests subdirectory of the Http directory located in the app folder, these allow us to validate the data that is sent and if used in a web application that uses forms the behavior will be that if the data is not valid (do not meet the restrictions that are set) the system returns to the previous page with and an object with errors is received, there is also a helper called old with which you can know the previous value of an input, Thanks to this we can implement that if a set of data does not meet the expectations it returns to the page with the form and with all the fields filled with the value that was sent, when a fomrRequest is used for an API request and the data does not meet the restrictions what is returned is a json object that has two attributes, the first one the error message and an array that in turn contains an associative array in which the index is the field name and the value is the error message related to this. We can validate from the existence of a field, if it will be of alphanumeric type or a number is expected, its size (you can specify a minimum and a maximum, in case of strings is its length and if it is numeric is its value) you can specify its shape (for example, if you want it to comply with the shape of an ip address) you can even use a regular expression to determine whether or not it has the expected values. We can also interact with a database or perform conditional validations, but in this text we will only see simple validations, in the case of the teacher in which the characteristics that we have determined will be name, username, password and height we will validate that a username is assigned, that this is not more than 8 characters and not less than 5, in the case of the height should be a number ranging between 1.5 and 2.10, the password that in this case another attribute will be requested to confirm it and this must be equal to it and the key field that must be confirmed.

The result of the above command is the class:

```
<?php

namespace App\HttpRequests;

use IlluminateFoundationHttpFormRequest;

class StoreDocenteRequest extends FormRequest
{
    /**
     * Determine if the user is authorized to make this request.
     *
     * @return bool
     */
    public function authorize()
    {
        return false;
    }
```

```
    /**
     * Get the validation rules that apply to the request.
     *
     * @return array<string, mixed>
     */
    public function rules()
    {
        return [
            //
        ];
    }
}
```

We will modify the authorize method to specify that we authorize the use of this validator, the rules method with the validation rules that will be in an associative array in which the indexes will correspond to the name of the field to validate and the value includes a string with one or more restrictions, in case of having several these are separated by the pipe symbol and if they have some parameter it is specified after a colon:

```
    public function rules()
    {
        return [
            'username' => 'required|min:5|max:8',
            'height' => 'required|numeric|min:1.5|max:2.10',
            'password' => 'required|confirmed'.
        ];
    }
```

In the case of key we need to add an entry with the name key_confirmation since the use of the confirmed constraint requires the existence of a field with the name <field>_confirmation and it will check that both values are equal. There is no messages method that will be responsible for providing error messages for each of the constraints that we specify, this function also returns an associative array in which the values contain the error message and the indexes correspond to the constraint to be evaluated, to specify are written in the form <field>.<restriction> thanks to this we can specify to which field is attributed, in the previous example both the user name and the height are required and if the key exists we must verify that it is correctly confirmed, the messages method would be:

```
public function messages()
{
  return [
    'username.required' => 'Username is required',
    'username.min' => 'Username must be at least 5 characters long',
    'username.max' => 'Username must be 8 characters or more',
    'height.required' => 'Height is required',
    'height.numeric' => 'Height must be numeric',
    'height.min' => 'The minimum height will be 1.5',
    'height.max' => 'The maximum height will be 2.10',
    'key.required' => 'Key is required',
    'key.confirmed' => 'The key must be confirmed',
  ];
}
```

But to be able to use it we must specify to the framework where it is located and that we do it if in the first lines, we write:

```
//// code to include liberias ...
use App\HttpRequestsStoreDocenteRequest;
//// code to include liberias ...
```

Depending on the context of use will be the way in which the FormRequest reacts, but in general we must inject it in the controller, that is to say to specify that the parameter is of that type, in the signature of the method, we must specify it this way:

```
public function store(StoreDocenteRequest $request)
{
    //// code to implement ...
}
```

If we are using forms then we must adapt them, ours would look like this:

```
@extends('templates.main')
@section('content')
<form action="{{route('teachers.store')}}" method='post' enctype='multipart/form-data'>
 @csrf
 <label for='name'>Name</label>
 <input type='text' name='name' id='name' value="{{old('name')}}">
 <br>
 <label for='UserName'>UserName</label>
 <input type='text' name='user_name' id='UserName' value="{{old('user_name')}}">
 <br>
 <label for='password'>User's password</label>.
 <input type='password' name='password' id='password' value="{{old('password')}}">
 <br>
 <label for='pwd'>Repeat the key</label>.
 <input type='password' name='clave_confirmation' id='pwd'>
 <br>
 <label for='image'>Image</label>
 <input type='file' name='image' id='image' value="{{old('image')}}">
 <br>
 <label for='height'>height</label>.
 <input type='text' name='height' id='height' value="{{old('height')}}">
 <br>
 <input type='submit' value='SAVE'>
</form>
@endsection
```

Within the template we have access to the object $errors that has several methods that can be useful: any that returns true or false depending if in the validation errors were found or not, there is also any that returns an indexed array[21] in which the error messages product of the validation are found and I can call the get method specifying the name of the field to know in an array all the messages that apply to this field.

Consuming the API

The action of making use of the API, processing the returned data (the json that was obtained) is known as consuming the API, there are two ways, from the same origin and from a different origin, in the first case requests are made to this from the views of the same system (really from JavaScript[22] whatever the origin always makes use of this language), it is possible to use various libraries (axios, jquery) or implement the API fetch (incorporated in HTML5 using JavaScript Vanilla).[23]

[21] In PHP, arrays can be associative or indexed, the latter use continuous integers in their index (the classic $a[0]=$a[1];) while the others can be accessed with words ($a['red']=$a['blue'];).

[22] Language that runs in the browser (this is why it is known as client-side) thanks to which interactivity can be obtained and dynamism can be added to web pages.

[23] The connotation of JavaScript Vanilla is given to the use of the language with its functionalities in a pure form without the help of any external library.

From the very beginning

For the first case we will make use of the AJAX technology that is acronym of Asynchronous Javascript And Xml, that is the result of joining several knowledge (at the moment instead of using xml is used json) and it is based on making HTTP requests from javascript that will give us how result data in json that are shown in elements of the page (elements of the DOM[24]), we can do this we will use the fetch of html5, in this case we will make a view that contains an input of type select to place in it the names of the teachers that we will obtain making a call to the method index of our api (the end point will be http://192.168.56.106:8001/api/teachers using the get method).

First, we will analyze the visible part (the body) of our page:

```
<body>
   <button onclick="load()">Load</button>
   List of teachers <select id="list"></select>
</body>
```

This code can be considered as any web page, but we have added two singularities, the first is the creation of what is known as a *listener* which is a function that is activated when an event happens (in this case we are saying that when you press the button is executed load) and on the other hand we assigned the id to the element that we want to manipulate through the DOM

We will see that the "strong" work is in the JavaScript part since we have only said that at the moment of pressing the button the load function is executed, so now we will analyze the header of our page:

```
<head>
   <title>List of teachers</title>.
   <script>
     function load() {

        fetch('http://192.168.56.106:8000/api/docentes')
        .then( function extract(answer){
           return answer.json()
        })
        .then( function process(data){
           for (i=0; i<data.length; i++){
              const option = document.createElement('option');
              option.textContent = "Teacher: " + data[i].name;
              option.value = data[i].id;
              const select = document.getElementById('list');
              select.appendChild(option);
           }
        });
     }
   </script>
</head>
```

To make the code more evident we have omitted to use features such as the arrow function or the map method of the data array. Let's proceed to explain that the use of fetch is a feature that natively allows to make http requests, in this example a GET request is made (since the method is not being specified) to the url (to the end point) http://192.168.56.106:8000/api/docentes and this returns a promise (promises is a JavaScript topic that if you are not clear it is advisable to be documented in the)

The then is called when the promise is resolved so we will receive the response to the HTTP request of type GET that we made in the fetch, this request is not directly on which we will work since in it travel the headers, the status code, as well as the data that in this case is what we are interested in, therefore the function extract is carried out that returns us only json content (the data that interests us), this in turn is a promise that is also taken care of in its own then inside which

[24] Document Object Model is the in-memory representation of a web page, all html elements are objects.

the function process is executed that will be to do something with the data and in this example it is to load the names in a select.
The function process receives the data (in this case it is an array that contains all the objects of type teacher) so it iterates for each one of them from 0 and for each one of them first creates an object of type option (remember that in html a select shows several options) assigns the text "Teacher: " accompanied by the name of each one and also sets the value for the option (in this case it will be the identifier of each one of them), then adds the option to the select that in our html we identify it as list.

What is normally obtained as a result of implementing actions like these is to raise the level of UX[25] but there are several frameworks and libraries that writing relatively little code allows to obtain a similar result, if we want to continue working with laravel it is possible to use livewire to create more dynamic user interfaces (views).

from a different origin

In the previous paragraph we commented that there are several frameworks such as Vue.js that are responsible for creating completely dynamic interfaces, this frameowrs only build client-side applications that are executed in the browser, commonly run on a different server, in the case of Vue.js as it is out of scope we will not explain its life cycle concepts, the concept of "components" is similar in both frameworks, is a part of the page, in vue.js we create a component which is called list.

```
<template>
  <button @click="cargarDocentes">Load teachers</button>.
  <select>
   <option v-for="docente in docentes" :key="docente.id" :value="docente.id">
Teacher: {{teacher.name}}
    </option>
  </select>
</template>

<script>
export default {
 data() {
  return {
   teachers: [],
  };
 },
 methods: {
   loadTeachers() {
     fetch('http://192.168.56.106:8000/api/docentes')
     .then(response => response.json())
     .then(data => {
       this.teachers = data;
     });
   },
 },
};
</script>
```

Similarly we see that it has two parts one that is similar to the template body of the previous example but this time we find an attribute @click="cargarDocentes"that the framework is indicating that when you click on this element (the button) is executed the function cargarDocentesthat is defined in the script part, similar there is also a part of script, in this one is defined among other things a function to call to the API and in this occasion if we make use of the arrow functions, but in the second one we see that in the body we are not creating the options in if what is done is that the data array was assigned to the teachers

[25] User experience (User Xperience) is how users interact with a product or service.

array, since in the template there is a v-for directive (this is specific of Vue.js) which iterates over an array.

8. Web Services

Web services (WS) are programs that are used by other programs since long ago people realized that computers could process data at higher speed and on a larger scale, so there was a great evolution in programming, even programs that are used by programs, today it is very common to interact with an artificial intelligence, which we feed with data and also get data, but for us to have reached this all started since the 1990s in which they begin, its characteristics are Interoperability, Abstraction, Security and Physical Independence.

There are different types of web services, from those based on SOAP, the REST FULL and GraphQL, those that are RPC, but all of them have a similar architecture to the basic communication model (exposed by Claude E. Shannon and Warren Weaver in their article A Mathematical Theory of Communication[3]), so it can be seen:

- Receiver: The server that publishes the web service.
- Sender: The customer who consumes the web service.
- Channel: It is the medium through which the information sent or received flows, it can be a protocol or a network and in this case it is commonly the HTTP protocol.
- Message: It is the Request/Response transmitted, it is the data that in case of SOAP based sw is stored in XML and in REST APIS it is handled in JSON.

At this moment the most common web services are of the REST FULL type.

RESTFull

Web services that respect the REST (Representational State Transfer) principles are considered a RestFull API, these guidelines were proposed by Roy Fielding in his PhD thesis in 2000, following these principles ensures compliance with the characteristics of a web service.

1. Principle of using a **client-server** architecture, this indicates that there is a separation of responsibilities between the client and the server, leaving the client responsible for the user experience while the server is in charge of processing the requests and the resources used.
2. A web service must be stateless, so each request sent to a server must contain the necessary information to generate the desired response.
3. Use of a **uniform interface** that allows its use without the need to create new forms of access.

Laravel makes it very easy to implement restful web services,

Works cited

[1] G. D. Campo, "Design Patterns, Refactoring and Antipatterns. Advantages and Disadvantages of their Use in Object-Oriented Software," *Cuadernos de Ingeniería,* vol. 4, no. 4, pp. 101-136, 22 09 2019.

[2] M. J. N. Cíceri Vazquez, Introduction to Laravel: Robust and Large-Scale Applications, 1st ed. ed.

[3] C. Shannon and W. Weaver, "A Mathematical Theory of Communication," *Bell System Technical Journal,* vol. 27, no. 3, p. 379-423, 1948.

Blog of https://kennyhorna.com/

laravel documentation: https://laravel.com/

laravel courses in :
https://rimorsoft.com/
https://styde.net/

Printed by Books on Demand GmbH, Norderstedt / Germany